Fate and Fortune

GEDDES & GROSSET

This edition published by Geddes & Grosset, an imprint of
Children's Leisure Products Limited

First published in this edition 1999

Cover photograph by Bozena Cannizzaro
courtesy of Telegraph Colour Library

ISBN 1 85534 284 7

Printed and bound in the UK

Contents

Astrology

History

Astrology is an ancient craft that has its origin in the mists of time. It is impossible to place accurately the beginnings, but one thing that is certain is that astrology began as a subject intimately combined with astronomy. Its history is therefore the history of astronomy until the two subjects parted company, a split that essentially began when Nicolai Copernicus (1473–1543) published his book *De revolutionibus*. In this book he postulated that, contrary to earlier thinking in which the Earth was the centre of the solar system, the Sun actually formed the focus about which all the planets orbited.

It is thought that there was some study of these subjects five to six thousand years ago when Chaldean priests made maps of the skies. The Chaldeans were the most ancient of the Babylonian peoples. It was believed that heavenly bodies exerted influence upon man and whatever could not be ascribed to man must be due to actions of the gods or the deities of the planets. Subsequent study of the solar system began as pure observation because records and other data for calculation simply did not exist. The Egyptian and Greek civilisations gave much to the theories and practice of astrology, although much remained unwritten. It is said that the Chaldeans instructed the priests of the Pharaohs in astrology, and monuments exist that show a working knowledge of the subject. This was around 400–350 BC. A little earlier, in Greece around the beginning of the sixth century BC, the philosopher Thales (*c*.643–*c*.546 BC) studied astronomy and astrology as did Pythagoras (569–470 BC) who was credited by Copernicus as the person who developed the theory that the Earth and other planets revolved around the Sun.

There were many other Greek students, notably: Plato; Hippocrates, who combined astrology with medical diagnosis; Hipparchus, the founder of observational astronomy, who in 134 BC discovered a new star; and Claudius Ptolemaeus (100–178AD). Ptolemy wrote the *Almagest*, which is a star catalogue of just over a thousand stars, and also a consideration of the motion of the Moon and the planets. He also wrote the *Tetrabiblos*, the earliest surviving book on astrology.

In Rome and the extended empire at this time, astrology was held in very high regard, and great faith was placed in the work and advice of astrologers who were appointed to the Emperors. The Moon was considered particularly influential and can be found depicted on many of their coins. Among the many Romans active in this field were Porphyry (232–304 AD), who is said to have developed the house method, and Julius Maternus (around 300 AD), who wrote a number of books on astrology.

From about 500 AD Arabs became the prime movers in science and philosophy, but by the early Middle Ages (the thirteenth century) interest was rekindled in Europe, at which time astrology had been divided into three distinct fields: *natural* or *mundane* astrology, which is prominent in forecasting national events, weather, etc; *horary* astrology, used to answer a question through the use of a chart drawn up for the actual time of asking; and *judicial* astrology, in which the fortune of an individual is determined by using a birth chart.

The fifteenth and sixteenth centuries in Europe saw the rise of several famous names, including the Polish astronomer Copernicus. Although Copernicus concurred with the views of Pythagoras, he could not prove the theory, and many attribute the real establishment of the principle (i.e. that the planets orbit the Sun) to Johannes Kepler (1571–1630), the German astronomer. The medieval precursor of chemistry was alchemy, and one famous practitioner was Phillipus Aureolus Paracelsus (1493–1541), who also had some astrological leanings. He believed that the Sun, planets and stars influenced people, whether for good or evil. From this era also came Nostradamus (1503–1566). Michael Nostradamus has become one of the most famous of astrologists and prophets, and he also studied medicine. Almost from the outset it was thought that medical knowledge must, by necessity, include an understanding of astrology.

The work of the Dane Tycho Brahe (1546–1601) could, in some respects, be considered a watershed in the study of astrology/astronomy. Brahe became an observer of the heavens and in so doing was recognised as the most accurate since Hipparchus, centuries before. He prepared tables, designed instruments and studied the motion of the planets, particularly Mars, and it was this initial work that led Kepler to formulate his famous laws of planetary motion. Kepler was assistant to Brahe when the latter moved to Prague following the death of his patron, King Frederick. Kepler's work proved to be pivotal in advancing the understanding of astronomy. Kepler compared the work of Ptolemy, Copernicus and Tycho Brahe to produce three laws:

1. The orbit of each planet is an ellipse with the Sun at one of the foci (an ellipse has two foci.)
2. A line drawn from a planet to the Sun sweeps out equal areas in equal times.
3. The squares of the sidereal periods (time taken to orbit the Sun, measured relative to the stars) are proportional to the cubes of the mean distances from the Sun.

Kepler believed that the stars exerted an influence upon events and that astrology could predict the most mundane of happenings. During the sixteenth and seventeenth centuries there were many famous names who combined astrology with astronomy, mathematics or, commonly, medicine. These included the Italian physicist Galileo Galilei, a French professor of mathematics and doctor of medicine, Jean Morin, an Italian monk and mathematician, Placidus de Tito, and in England, William Lilly, who became famous as a practitioner of horary astrology and accurately predicted the Great Fire of London in 1666.

The poet John Dryden used astrology in predicting numerous events in his own life and the lives of his sons, including both their deaths. Following Dryden's own death in 1700, although not because of it, astrological practice declined on the continent but flourished in England. This influence extended to France at the start of the nineteenth century, where a sound scientific basis to the subject was sought.

William Allan (1800–1917), otherwise known as Alan Leo, was considered by many to be the father of modern astrology. He lectured widely throughout England and edited a magazine called *Modern Astrology*. He was also a professional astrologer and a prolific author on the subject, writing 30 books. In 1915 he founded the Astrological Lodge of London. Although the war years were disruptive to the study and practice of astrology, a large following was developed in North America. However, continental Europe suffered during the Second World War as Hitler's forces caused wholesale destruction, and Hitler himself, unhappy with adverse astrological predictions, destroyed books and records and incarcerated unfortunate practitioners.

Today astrology holds interest for many people, and growing numbers are becoming fascinated by its study. However, there is a dichotomy between astrology and astronomy.

The solar system

The early visualisations of the heavens and the stars showed the Earth at the centre of a large revolving sphere. It was thought that the stars seen in the sky were somehow fastened onto the inner surface of this sphere. The stars that appeared to revolve around the Earth but did not move in relation to each other were called the 'fixed stars'. Among the many fixed stars there are some in particular that have certain characteristics and that can be used in astrological charts. For example, Regulus (or Alpha Leonis) is the brightest star in the constellation of Leo and signifies pride, good luck and success.

From early times it was noted that while many stars remained fixed, five in particular did not, and these wandered about the sky. These were the planets of the solar system because at that time not all eight remaining planets (other than Earth) had been identified. The discovery of Uranus, Neptune and Pluto followed the invention of the telescope, and Uranus was the first planet so observed, in 1781.

For the purposes of astrology, the Sun, which is actually a star, is considered as a planet. It is approximately 150 million kilometres from Earth and has a diameter of 1.4 million kilometres. Energy is generated in the core, from nuclear fusion, where the temperature is about fifteen million degrees.

The planets

The Moon is a satellite of Earth but for convenience is also treated as a planet. It orbits the Earth roughly every 27 days, and the same face is always kept towards Earth, lit by light reflected from the Sun. The Moon seems to change size – the process known as waxing and waning – and it is called 'new' when it is situated between the Earth and the Sun and, because it is not illuminated, cannot be seen. The full Moon occurs about 14 days later, when the full face is totally illuminated.

Planets with their orbits between the Sun and the Earth's orbit are called 'inferior'. There are two planets in this category, Mercury and Venus. Mercury is the smallest planet in the solar system and takes 88 Earth days to complete one orbit, rotating slowly on its axis, and taking 58 Earth days for one revolution. Its elliptical orbit is eccentric, varying in distance from the Sun from 47 to 70 million kilometres.

Venus is the brightest planet seen from Earth and is known as the morning or evening star. It is about 108 million kilometres from the Sun and has a diameter similar to Earth's, at 12,300 kilometres. Venus spins very slowly on its axis, and a day is equivalent to 24.3 Earth days, and a year is 225 days. It is unusual in being the only planet to revolve in the opposite direction to the path of its orbit.

The remaining planets, from Mars to Pluto, are called the 'superior planets', being on the distant side of Earth from the Sun.

Mars takes about 687 Earth days to complete an orbit, and a day is just a fraction longer than one Earth day. The surface is solid and mainly red in colour because of the type of rock. There are many surface features, some of which are attributed to the action of water, although none is found there now. Mars is sometimes a dominant feature of the night sky, particularly when it occasionally approaches nearer to Earth, and it has from ancient times exerted considerable fascination.

Jupiter is the largest and heaviest planet in the solar system and has a diameter of 142,800 kilometres. The planet gives out more energy than it receives from the Sun and must therefore have an internal energy source. It is due, in part, to this that the atmosphere is seen to be in steady movement. Parallel bands of colour are seen, but a particularly noticeable feature is the Great Red Spot, which is thought to be an enormous storm, larger than Earth, coloured red because of the presence of phosphorus. The magnetic field of Jupiter is thousands of times stronger than Earth's, and radio waves emanate from the planet. Jupiter has 18 satellites, or moons, of which four are called the 'Galilean satellites' – Io, Europa, Ganymede and Callisto – because they were first seen by Galileo in 1610. There are three other groups of satellites, of which the innermost contains Adastrea, Amalthea, Metis and Thebe.

The next planet out from the Sun is Saturn, the second largest in the solar system. It has a diameter of 120,800 kilometres and the orbit takes 29 Earth years at a distance of 1507 million kilometres from the Sun. Because of its rapid rotation, Saturn is flattened at the poles with a consequent bulging at its equator. A day lasts for a little over 10 hours, and the surface temperature is -170 degrees Celsius. The most obvious and interesting feature of Saturn is its rings, which consist of ice, dust and rock debris, and some of which may have derived from the break-up of a satellite. The rings are about a quarter of a million kilometres across, and there are three main ones but hundreds of smaller ones.

Saturn also has 24 satellites, or moons, of which Titan is the largest with a diameter of 5200 kilometres (larger than Mercury). Some moons were discovered by the Voyager spacecraft in 1989, including Atlas, Calypso and Prometheus.

The planets Mercury through to Saturn were all known to astrologers and astronomers for many years. The remaining planets, Uranus, Neptune and Pluto, were discovered only in modern times, after the advent of the telescope. These are therefore often called the 'modern planets' by astrologers.

Uranus is 50,080 kilometres in diameter and a day lasts 17 hours while a year is equivalent to 84 Earth years. Because of its tilted axis, some parts of the planet's surface are in light for about 40 years and then in darkness for the remainder of its year. Uranus was discovered by William Herschel in 1781 but was something of a mystery until 1986 and the approach of Voyager. It has a faint ring system and 15 moons, some of which are very small indeed (less than 50 kilometres in diameter).

Neptune was discovered in 1846, but its existence was earlier correctly postulated because of observed irregularities in the orbit of Uranus. It takes 165 Earth years to complete an orbit and is almost 4.5 billion kilometres from the Sun. It is 17 times the mass of Earth and has a diameter at its equator of 48,600 kilometres. There are three rings and eight known satellites, the largest of which, Titan, is similar in size to the Earth's Moon.

Pluto, the smallest and most distant planet from the Sun, had its existence predicted because of its effect on the orbits of Neptune and Uranus and was finally discovered in 1930, although little is known about it. A day is equivalent to almost seven days on Earth, and a year is nearly 249 Earth years. Pluto has a very wide elliptical orbit, which brings it closest to the Sun (its *perihelion*) once in each orbit. Because of its great distance from the Sun (7.4 billion kilometres at its maximum), the surface temperature is very low, about 230 degrees. In 1979, one small moon, called Charon, was discovered, but since it is about one quarter the size of Pluto itself, the two act almost as a double planet system.

A few technicalities

As has been mentioned, the orbits of the planets are elliptical rather than circular, and there is a degree of eccentricity as well. When viewed from Earth, this combination of factors produces what may appear to be peculiar effects. For example, planets may move around the sky, slow and then appear to move backwards for a time. This apparent backward motion is called *retrograde motion* and is simply caused by the Earth moving more quickly through its orbit in comparison to another planet. It *seems* as though the planet being observed is moving backwards, but in reality it is moving forwards, albeit in the line of sight at a slower rate. It is similar to a fast train moving alongside a slow train, which makes the latter appear to be moving backwards. In astronomical tables *R* denotes retrograde while *D* marks a return to direct motion.

Another astronomical parameter used in astrology is that of conjunctions. A *conjunction* is when two or more planets (including the Sun of course) are in a line when viewed from Earth.

Conjunction

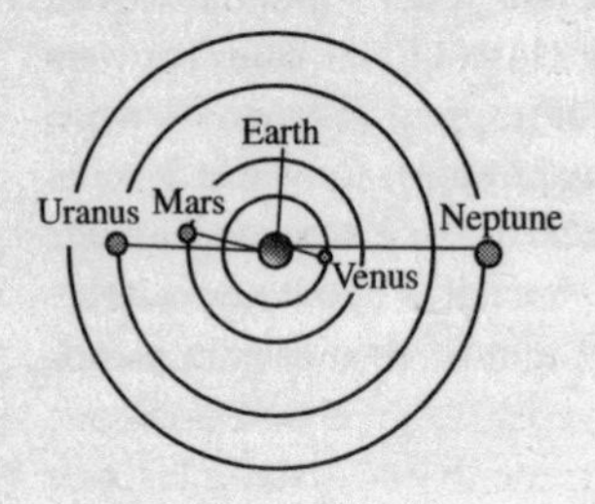

Mars in opposition to the sun

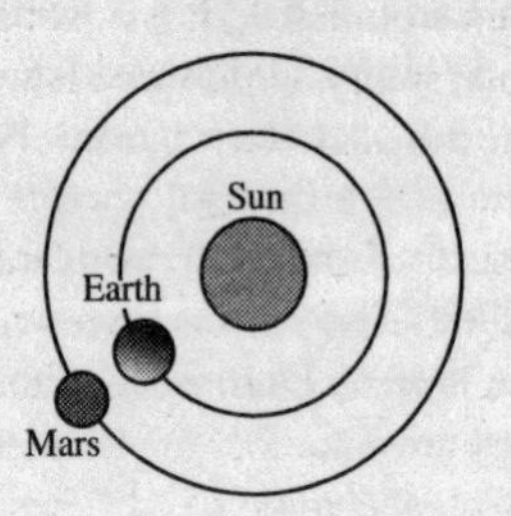

Mars in superior conjunction

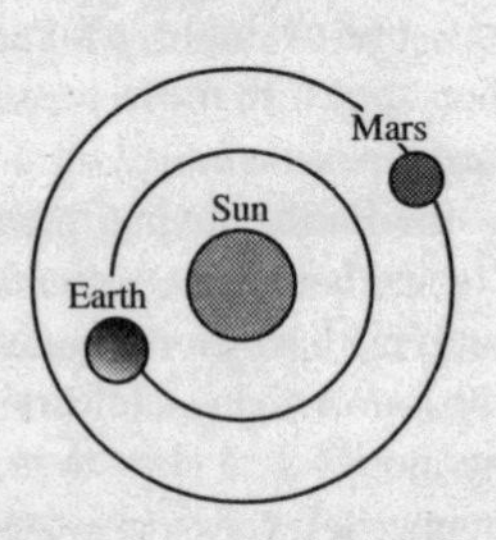

Mercury and Venus in superior conjunction

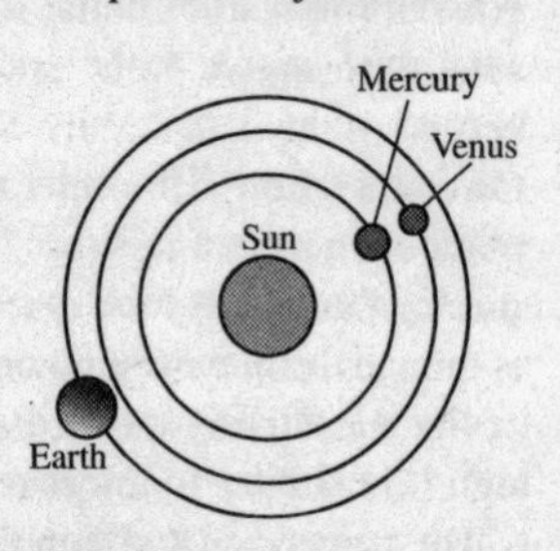

Conjunctions

On occasion, Earth, Venus and the Sun will all be in a straight line. If Venus is between Earth and the Sun it is called an 'inferior conjunction'. If, however, Venus is on the other side of the Sun from Earth, it is a 'superior conjunction'. The same applies to Mercury. *Opposition* is when, for example, Earth lies between the Sun and Mars; then Mars is in opposition. Opposition is when one of the superior planets (all except Mercury, Venus and, of course, Earth) is opposite the Sun in the sky, i.e. making an angle of 180 degrees when viewed from Earth (*see* figure opposite).

Of vital significance to the correct interpretive study of astrology are a number of parameters that enable the relative positions of planets to be fixed. These include the three great circles, one of which is the ecliptic, and the Zodiac. (A great circle is essentially any circle projected onto the celestial sphere whose plane passes through the centre of the Earth.) The horizon and celestial equator (the Earth's equator projected outward onto the celestial sphere) form two great circles, and the ecliptic is the third. The *ecliptic* is the path that the Sun apparently forms in the heavens. Of course the Earth orbits the Sun, but it seems from Earth to mark out a path that lies at an angle to the celestial equator. This means that the two lines cross twice, at the vernal and autumn equinoxes, otherwise known as the March equinox (or first point of the sign Aries) and September equinox (or first point of the sign Libra). (*See* figure overleaf)

The two points at which the ecliptic is farthest from the celestial equator are called the solstices, and these occur in June for the summer solstice (when the Sun enters Cancer) and December for the winter solstice (on entering Capricorn). In the southern hemisphere these equinoxes and solstices mark the reverse situation.

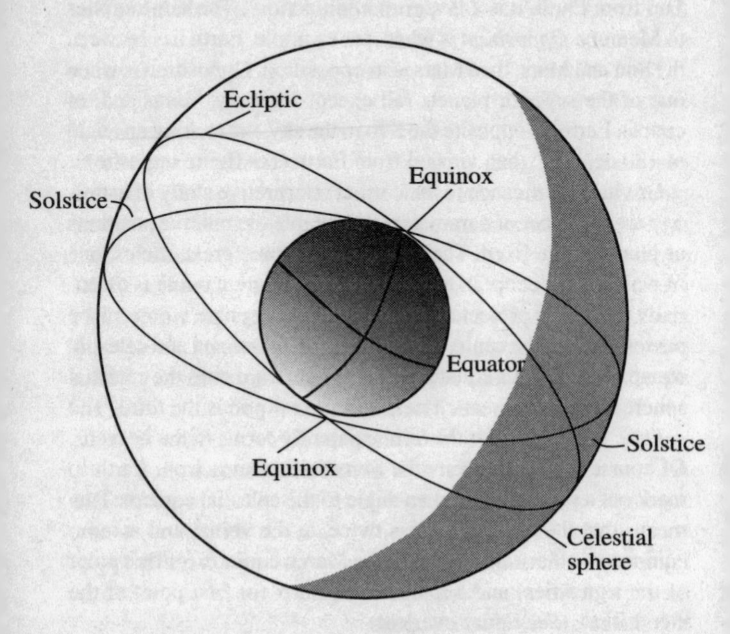

The ecliptic and the celestial sphere

The ecliptic itself is divided into twelve equal divisions, each of 30 degrees, one for each Zodiac sign. As the Sun apparently moves around the Earth, it goes from one sign of the Zodiac to the next. A person's Sun sign is the sign before which the Sun seems to be at the time of birth.

The *Zodiac* is a 'band' in the heavens that extends to seven or eight degrees on either side of the ecliptic. Within this band, or path, are contained the apparent movements of the planets, except Pluto. The solar system can be considered as a relatively planar feature, and within this plane the Earth revolves around the Sun. The planes of the orbits of all the other planets are within seven degrees of Earth's, save for Pluto, which is nearer 17 degrees. The Zodiac is then split into twelve segments of 30 degrees, one for each sign of the Zodiac and each represented by a particular star constellation (*see* the figure overleaf). These signs are essentially a means of naming the sections of the sky within which the planets move. The constellation names, Scorpio, Libra, etc, have no significance although they are bound up in the development of the subject. It should be noted that today, the 30-degree segments no longer coincide with the constellation because of a phenomenon called *precession of the equinoxes*. Precession results in the Earth's axis of rotation not remaining in the same position but forming a cone shape traced out in space. It is due to the gravitational pulls of the Sun and Moon producing a turning force, or torque. This occurs only because the Earth bulges at the equator – a perfect sphere would not be affected. The Earth takes almost 26,000 years (known as the Great Year) to sweep out the cone, and in astrology the point Aries 0 degrees (the First Point of Aries), where the celestial equator cuts the ecliptic, moves with time. Because of precession, the equator

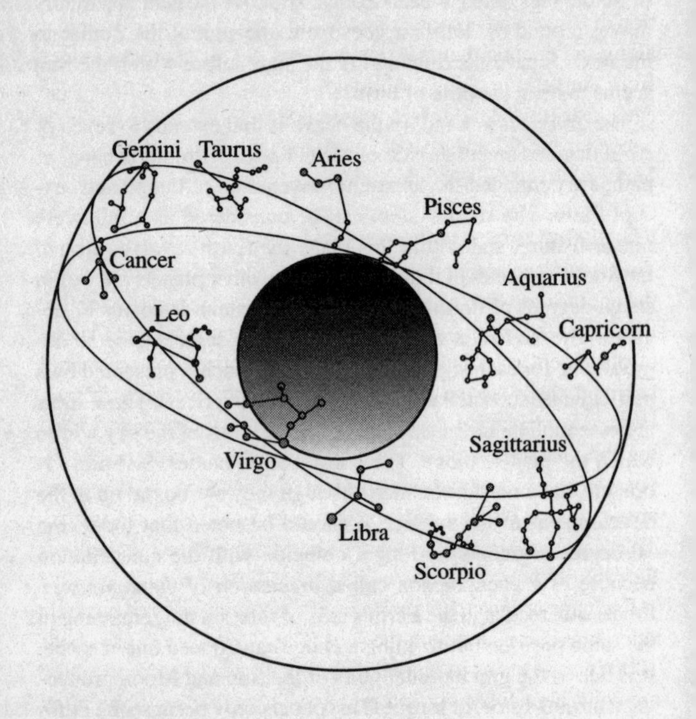

The constellations

crossing-point moves around the ecliptic, and now the First Point of Aries (the vernal equinox of astronomy) lies in the constellation of Pisces and is soon to move into Aquarius. The 30 degrees along the ecliptic that is Aries remains the 30 degrees counted from the vernal equinox, although that equinox is farther back each year (this is, therefore, retrograde motion). Aries has been considered the first sign from hundreds of years BC, when it was believed that the Earth had a birthday.

The Great Year

The Great Year, as mentioned, is divided into twelve periods when the equinox is taken to be against each of the constellations that lie around the ecliptic. This is by no means an accurate division or placement, and the beginning of each period, or age, cannot be fixed easily as the constellations overlap and vary in size. However, each age is taken to be about 2000 years, and by tracing the characteristics of each age in history a pattern can be constructed. From available historical details, the last 2000 years are typified as Piscean and the 2000 years before that as Taurean. This links with the precession of the equinoxes mentioned earlier, and so the next period will be the *Age of Aquarius*.

Each age of the Great Year identified this far has certain characteristics associated with the sign. The *Age of Leo* began about 10000 BC and has as its animal representative the lion, with which are connected creativity and regality. The Sun is its planet. It is interesting to note the early attempts at art, by way of prehistoric cave paintings, and of course the vital importance of the Sun in those times.

The *Age of Cancer* (8000–6000 BC) is associated with the traits of home and family. At this time human beings began building dwellings, and some carvings symbolising fertility have been found from this period.

From 6000 to 4000 BC was the *Age of Gemini*, which represents a sign of intellectual capacity. It is thought that writing began in some form during this Age, hence communication, a further characteristic of Gemini, became important. Civilisation developed apace with cuneiform writing by the end of the Age, and it is possible that human beings had begun to travel and explore.

The *Age of Taurus* followed, from 4000 to 2000 BC, and there are numerous instances that relate to the Taurean features of solidity and security with beauty. These traits are seen in the Egyptian dynasties and the worship of the bull, and in the enormous and ornate temples and the pyramids.

The next age is that of *Aries* (2000 BC–0 AD). Aggressive and assertive qualities are associated with Aries, as are physical fitness and supremacy. These are balanced by courage and also harmony. All these characteristics are well exemplified by the Greeks, who dominated in battle and architecture and yet created the first democratic government. The symbol of the ram found an outlet in numerous ways, including as an emblem of the Roman army.

We are currently in the *Age of Pisces* (0–2000 AD), albeit towards the end of the period. It began with the birth of Christ, and there are numerous connections to the sign of the fish at this time. The secret symbol for the early Christians was the fish, Jesus was called *Ichthus*, the fish, and many of his disciples were fishermen. Qualities such as kindness, charity and forgiveness are typical, as is selflessness, although an element of confusion can also be discerned. We are on the brink of the new Age, that of *Aquarius* (2000–4000 AD), but in many respects the signs are already there to be seen. Aquarian influence can be seen in the strong presence of science and technology and space travel. Also Aquarian is a sense of detachment and of being impersonal.

Signs and symbols

Each sign of the Zodiac has a particular graphical representation, called a glyph, which relates to an animal or something similar. The same applies to the planets, and these symbols are used , with others, in constructing an astrological chart.

Symbol	Sign	Representation	Name
♈	Aries	the ram's horns	The Ram
♉	Taurus	the bull's head	The Bull
♊	Gemini	two children	The Twins
♋	Cancer	breasts	The Crab
♌	Leo	the heart, or the lion's tail	The Lion
♍	Virgo	the female genitalia	The Virgin
♎	Libra	a pair of scales	The Balance
♏	Scorpio	the male genitalia	The Scorpion
♐	Sagittarius	the Centaur's arrow	The Archer
♑	Capricorn	a goat's head and fish's tail	The Goat
♒	Aquarius	waves of water or air	The Water-bearer
♓	Pisces	two fish	The Fishes

The glyphs of the planets are as follows:

Planet	Symbol	Planet	Symbol
Sun	○	Jupiter	♃
Moon	☽	Saturn	♄
Mercury	☿	Uranus	♅
Venus	♀	Neptune	♆
Mars	♂	Pluto	♇

These planetary symbols are all made up of essentially the same elements, the cross, half-circle and circle, all in different combinations. These pictorial representations are linked with the very early days of human beings, when communication was achieved using such graphical methods. As such, these elements each have a particular significance:

- the circle represents eternity, something without end, the spirit;
- a dot inside a circle represents the spirit or power beginning to come out;
- the cross represents the material world;
- and the semicircle stands for the soul.

The signs of the Zodiac

The signs appear to have got their names from the depths of history and prehistory, and do not necessarily concur with their astronomical counterparts, the constellations. In some civilisations, the signs were attributed to parts of the body. The likeliest race to have adopted this were the Greeks, who also linked the signs to various plants.

Aries – the head
Libra – the kidneys
Taurus – the throat
Scorpio – genitalia
Gemini – hands and arms
Sagittarius – hips and thighs
Cancer – the breasts
Capricorn – the knee
Leo – the heart
Aquarius – calf and ankle
Virgo – the intestines
Pisces – the feet

Below are given the main features of the signs of the Zodiac, and these will be followed later by a fuller description of the character and personal details associated with the various sun signs, i.e. when the Sun passes through each of the signs as it appears to move on the ecliptic.

Aries

The astrological new year occurs around 21 March, when the Sun enters Aries, and this new aspect is mirrored in typical Arian traits of energy, keenness and enthusiasm. The Arian can be something of a pioneer and thus somewhat self-centred with a selfish streak. Aries is the most personal of the signs.

Taurus

Taureans seek and reflect stability, security, and are generally practical with a possessive side to their character. Risks will be taken only if they are absolutely essential, and even then it will be only after a great deal of careful thought. In general Taureans are trustworthy and pleasant and yet unenterprising, which in some may lead to them become a little boring.

Gemini

This third sign of the Zodiac is that of the heavenly twins, which, not surprisingly, can surface as a certain duality, which in a negative sense may result in someone being two-faced. Geminians are intelligent, quick of mind, versatile, and are often good communicators. If the dual nature is too strongly negative then it may lead to a lack of achievement through being over-committed and trying to do too many things at once.

Cancer

Changeable, sympathetic, kind, hard on the outside but easily hurt or offended, emotional and devoted – a home and family builder. These are all Cancerian traits and paint an essentially sensitive picture but with the strengths of devotion and faithfulness. Intellectually, Cancerians are very intuitive and have a strong imagination. If these traits are over-stressed or misused, it can lead to restlessness and over-worry.

Leo

Leo is the only sign ruled by the Sun and, like the lion, so-called king of the beasts, the Leonian can be regal, dignified and magnanimous. They are faithful, trusting but strong-willed, with fixed principles and ideas, and yet if carried too far this may result in bossiness. Similarly, someone may become snobbish, conceited and domineering.

Virgo

Virgoans are typically worker types; they dislike a leading role in anything, and yet they are intellectually very capable, although with a tendency to worry. In work and at home they pay attention to detail with precision and clarity. Closeness to others may be avoided, resulting in the perception among others of Virgoans keeping to themselves, which in turn may be misinterpreted as inhospitality.

Libra

This seventh sign of the Zodiac is opposite to Aries, which makes Librans interested in relating to a partner. As such they tend to be companionable, tactful and like to be in pleasant surroundings. Librans are often unfairly dubbed as lazy. They may also have a tendency to be quite aggressive. A Libran may be of the type who sits on the fence over an issue and, seeing both sides of an argument, may be impossibly indecisive.

Scorpio

This sign is one of intense energy, with deep, passionate feelings about the object of their attention, be it a person or an issue. Scorpions can be passionate, but in excess this can result in resentment, jealousy and even hatred. However, they can equally be warm and charming, and their virtues become apparent when dealing with real life rather than more trivial matters.

Sagittarius

In the earlier days of astrology, Sagittarius was always represented by a man joined to a horse, signifying the duality of the sign – a combination of strength and intelligence. Sagittarians are often intellectuals with a thirst for a challenge and an ability of body and mind to match. Taken to extremes, these traits can mean restlessness, carelessness, extravagance and a tendency to 'horseplay'.

Capricorn

Capricornians tend to be practical, ambitious and caring, and they often possess an excellent sense of humour. In personal relationships caution is their watchword but once decided they will make good partners. Capricornians are also traditionalists and excel in routine work or in organisational capacities. On the negative side, they may become too mean and stern, and caution may turn into selfishness.

Aquarius

Aquarians are typically independent and individualistic, and also friendly. Indeed, friendships once formed tend to be faithful, although contact with others can be rather impersonal. The freedom required by an Aquarian makes them paradoxical when it comes to love. However, the enquiring mind and originality is seen to good effect in pursuit of art or working in science and technology. An excess of Aquarian traits produces someone who is rebellious, tactless and eccentric.

Pisces

The last sign of the Zodiac, Pisces, is typified by a sensitivity that may border on the inhibited unless encouraged. Pisceans can be inspired and highly intuitive, although this may be clouded by mood swings, from elation to depression. Kindness is a common trait, and there is often a strong spiritual faith. In excess, Piscean characteristics may result in muddled thinking, weakness of character and excessive worry.

Groups of the Zodiac and rulings

The twelve signs of the Zodiac are traditionally subdivided into a number of groups. The members of each group share certain characteristics that in terms of chart interpretation provide additional information rather than primary details.

Triplicities

The first grouping is the *triplicities*, otherwise known as the elements, and consists of the signs for fire, earth, air and water. Aries, Leo and Sagittarius are the *fire triplicity*. This sign is represented by a keenness and enthusiasm and a tendency literally to burn with excitement. Often more sensitive people will be considered slow and dealt with impatiently. While people with the fire sign may be lively and exuberant, their fault will often be that they are too lively. However, such tendencies are likely to be offset, to some extent, by features elsewhere in a chart.

The *earth triplicity* contains Taurus, Virgo and Capricorn and, as might be expected, people with this sign are 'down to earth', although the earth sign is not totally dominant. However, the beneficial aspects include practicality and caution, and although considered dull by livelier people, there is a reassuring solidity and trustworthiness about people with this sign.

Gemini, Libra and Aquarius form the *air triplicity*, and communication is one of the key attributes. An 'ideas person' would have this sign prominent in his or her chart, but a potential fault can be that schemes and ideas occupy too much time at the expense of productivity. In addition, such people can be dismissive of sensitivity or caution in others.

The final triplicity is that of *water*, and it contains Cancer, Scor-

Pisces. Such people are naturally sensitive and intuitive, and often inspired, while also emotional and protective. Such people tend to be cautious of those with strong personalities, and their own faults may result from being too emotional.

It is often the case that people who have a shared strength in these signs will be compatible. Reference to the elements produces obvious attractions:

Fire air fans the flames while water puts them out and earth smothers them.

Earth water refreshes it while air and fire dry it out.

Air fire responds to air, while earth and water restrict it.

Water earth holds it, but air and fire diminish it.

Quadruplicities

The *quadruplicities* (otherwise known as qualities) form the second grouping. In this case the signs of the Zodiac are divided into three groups of four. The three qualities are 'cardinal', 'fixed' and 'mutable'. Aries, Libra, Cancer and Capricorn are of the *cardinal quadruplicity*. People with this sign dominant in their chart are outgoing and tend to lead. Taurus, Scorpio, Leo and Aquarius are of the *fixed quadruplicity*, which implies stability and a resistance to change. The *mutable quadruplicity* includes the remaining signs, Gemini, Sagittarius, Virgo and Pisces, and all have an adaptability. They often appear selfless.

The third grouping is into positive and negative (otherwise known as masculine and feminine). In essence these are descriptive rather than definitive terms and equate in a general sense to being self-expressive or extrovert (positive) on the one hand and receptive or introvert on the other. This does not mean that if a woman has a masculine sign she is not to be considered feminine, and vice versa.

The signs of the Zodiac and the three groupings

Taking into account the three groupings, the Zodiac signs are as follows:

Aries – fire, cardinal, masculine
Taurus – earth, fixed, feminine
Gemini – air, mutable, masculine
Cancer – water, cardinal, feminine
Leo – fire, fixed, masculine
Virgo – earth, mutable, feminine
Libra – air, cardinal, masculine
Scorpio – water, fixed, feminine
Sagittarius – fire, mutable, masculine
Capricorn – earth, cardinal, feminine
Aquarius – air, fixed, masculine
Pisces – water, mutable, feminine

Polarity

When interpreting charts, another useful link between signs is *polarity*. This is the relationship between a sign and the opposite sign across the Zodiac. Thus, on a circular display of the twelve signs, Aries is opposite Libra, Cancer opposite Capricorn, Taurus opposite Scorpio, etc. The signs thus opposed do not, however, have opposite tendencies; rather, the polar signs complement each other.

Before turning to the concept of ruling planets, it will be helpful to consider a few other definitions and some lines and angles that are critical in the construction of a chart. The *ascendant* is defined as the degree of a sign (or the ecliptic) that is rising above the horizon at an individual's birth and marks the junction of the first sign. This is essentially the beginning for any astrological chart construction and interpretation, and after calculation is marked on the chart, working clockwise upwards from the horizon line, which runs east-west across the chart. The ascendant is very significant and can only be constructed if a birth time is known. The significance of the ascendant is that it indicates the beginning of the personality and how an individual faces the world – his or her true self. There are many other factors that may lessen the influence of the ascendant sign, but if some characteristic comes out of a chart that reinforces one linked to the ascendant, then it will be a very significant trait.

The *descendant* is the point opposite to the ascendant, at 180 degrees to it, and is always the cusp, or junction, of the seventh house. Although it may often be left out of charts, the descendant is meant to indicate the sort of partner, friends, etc, with whom one associates and feels comfortable.

The *midheaven* is often abbreviated to MC, from the Latin *medium coeli*. At the time when one particular sign of the Zodiac is appearing over the horizon (the ascendant) there will inevitably be another sign that is at its greatest height. This sign is then said to culminate at the upper meridian of the appropriate place – in brief, the midheaven is the intersection of the meridian with the ecliptic at birth. The significance of the midheaven is that it relates to the career of an individual and the way in which it is pursued. It can also provide a general indication of aims and intentions and the type of partner that may be sought. The point opposite to the midheaven is the *imum coeli* and is connected to the subject's origins, his or her early and late life, and parental/domestic circumstances. The *imum coeli*, or IC, is sometimes referred to as the nadir, but strictly speaking this is incorrect. The nadir is actually a point in the heavens that is directly opposite the zenith, which itself is a point in the heavens directly over any place.

Influence of the planets

Every sign of the Zodiac has what is called a *ruling planet*, which is the planet that rules the ascendant sign. From the list below, it can be seen that if someone has Pisces rising, the ruling planet will be Neptune. Each planet rules one sign, save for Venus and Mercury, which each rule two. Of course, before William Herschel discovered Uranus in 1781 there were only seven planets (including the Sun and Moon) and therefore three further planets ruled two signs; Saturn ruled Aquarius in addition to Capricorn, Jupiter ruled Pisces in addition to Sagittarius, and Mars ruled Scorpio in addition to Aries.

There are also a number of planets that are termed personal. The *personal planets* are the Sun and Moon (which are always personal), the planet that rules the ascendant sign (called the chart ruler). The Sun ruler is the planet that rules the Sun sign, and the planet that rules the sign occupied by the Moon is called the Moon ruler.

These different rulings were established a long time ago. There are additional features and weightings given to the rulings, known as *exaltation, detriment* and *fall*. Each planet is exalted when it is in a particular sign from which it works well and with which there is a notable similarity, resulting in more significance being attributed to it in an interpretation. The exaltations are also listed below:

Planet	Ruling in	Exalted in	Detrimental in	Fall
Sun	Leo	Aries	Aquarius	Libra
Moon	Cancer	Taurus	Capricorn	Scorpio
Mercury	Gemini and Virgo	Virgo	Sagittarius	Pisces
Venus	Taurus and Libra	Pisces	Aries	Virgo
Mars	Aries	Capricorn	Libra	Cancer
Jupiter	Sagittarius	Cancer	Gemini	Capricorn
Saturn	Capricorn	Libra	Cancer	Aries
Uranus	Aquarius	Scorpio	Leo	Taurus
Neptune	Pisces	Leo	Virgo	Aquarius
Pluto	Scorpio	Virgo	Taurus	Pisces

The ruling planets and relationships

Opposing the ruling sign of the Zodiac, each planet also has a sign of detriment. In this the planet is said to be debilitated. Finally, in this section comes the sign opposite to exaltation, which is called the fall sign. This is the sign opposite to the sign of exaltation and, is where the planet is thought to be weak. (*See* list above).

The houses of the chart

The astrological chart is divided into houses – in effect this is a way of subdividing the space around the Earth. There are numerous such systems, which have been devised over the years and which fall into three groups: the Equal House System; the Quadrant System; and a variation on these systems.

The *Equal House System* is one of the oldest and after a period of disuse is now back in favour. The ecliptic is divided into twelve equal parts, and the houses are marked by great circles that meet at the poles of the ecliptic and start by going through the degree of the ecliptic ascending over the horizon, and then through every point 30 degrees farther around.

The main *Quadrant Systems* are called after the people who developed them, for example, Campanus, Regromontanus and Placidus, and appeared in the thirteenth, fourteenth and fifteenth centuries respectively. The system of Placidus was used almost exclusively until the early 1950s because it was the only system with published reference tables. It was, however, the only system that did not utilise great circles as the boundaries of the houses.

The final system, a variation, includes the system of Porphyry, which has its origins in antiquity. This is based on the Quadrant System, producing four unequal divisions that are each then equally divided into three.

The Equal House System is probably the simplest to use, and in it each house has a certain relevance or significance, affecting a particular aspect of life. The first six houses are concerned with a personal application while the last six apply more to one's dealings with other people and matters outside the home and family. There follows an expanded though not comprehensive description of each house, stipulating the association of the house with sign and planet and the resulting meanings. In this context, the planets stand for the provision of an impetus;

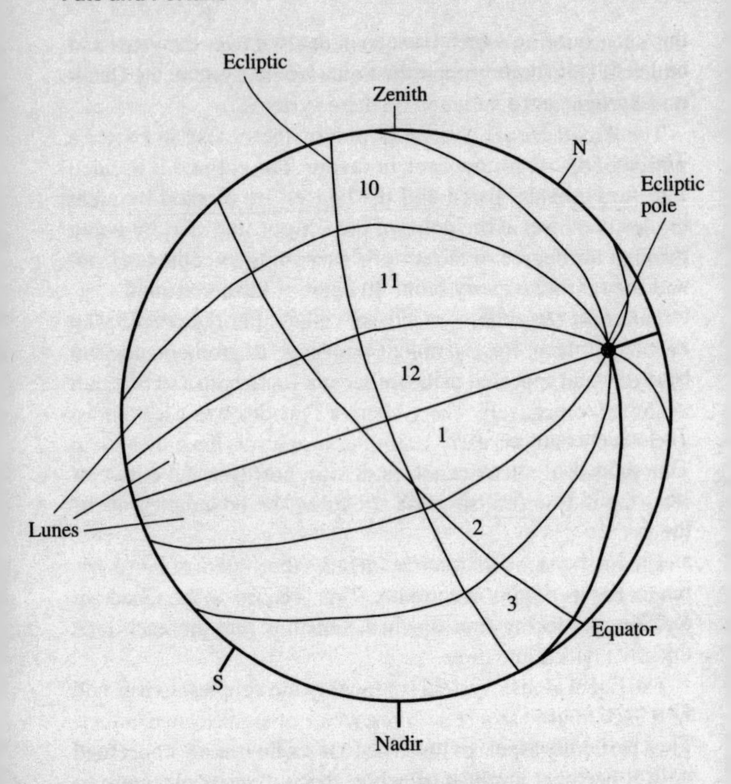

The Equal House system

the signs show how and where that impetus or motivation is to be used; and the houses indicate in which aspect of life the result will be seen.

The first house

This house is associated with Aries and the planet Mars, and because it includes the ascendant, or rising sign, is the most important house of the birth chart. This house refers to the person, which may include such factors as physical characteristics, nature, health, ego and so on. Planets within eight degrees of the ascendant will strongly affect all aspects of the person, including behaviour.

The second house

The second house is associated with Taurus and the planet Venus, and is concerned with the possessions and feelings of the person. As such, this house reflects attitudes to money, and since money and love are intimately entwined, this aspect will be of relevance when interpreting a chart. The second house is also concerned with priorities and the growth of things.

The third house

This is the house of Gemini and the planet Mercury, which not surprisingly means a concern for siblings and also neighbours. Other matters of a local nature, such as schooling, local travel and everyday matters of business, fall under this house. Mental attitude, also falls into the third house, meaning that many important patterns of behaviour, can be considered here. Decisions such as where to live and personal environment are typical examples. All aspects of communication also fall within this house. For anyone who is lost as to what decision to take, a positive influence from the third house will help him or her.

The fourth house

The sign of Cancer and the Moon are associated with the fourth house. The key concerns of this house are the home itself, home circumstances and the family, and caring for someone or something. The mother, or a mother figure, is a particularly strong feature of this house. The concept of the home and the protective enclosing also has analogy with the womb and the grave – thus, the beginning and end of life are also concerns.

The fifth house

This house is very different from the fourth, and the association of Leo and the Sun makes it the house of pleasure and creativity. This includes all such aspects, whether they be related to art, authors, games, gambling, and other leisure pursuits. Moving into the more personal sphere, the fifth house also accounts for lovers and love affairs, probably on a superficial level rather than a lasting, deep relationship. The other personal manifestation of creativity, that of producing children, and parents' feelings about children and procreation, fall under the rule of this house.

The sixth house

The sixth house is the last that impinges upon the person and personal acts, behaviour and relationships. Its sign is Virgo and the planet is Mercury. This is a very functional house, referring as it does to work of a routine nature, health and similar matters. The work may be in the work place, hence it also relates to employers, or at home in the daily round of chores. The concern of health also includes diet, and this house will help to assess the need and timing for a change.

The seventh house

The last six houses refer to the wider influences of one's life and to outward application. Libra and the planet Venus are associated with the seventh house, and the fundamental concern is with relationships with others. This house concerns commitment in partnership and can reflect the likely type of partner sought. It can also relate to the establishment of a business or the employment of new people, from the viewpoint of personal interaction. Because this house encompasses dealings with others, it can also include hostility and conflict.

The eighth house

This house, the opposite of the second, is associated with Scorpio and Pluto, and refers to possessions gained through others, whether as gifts or legacies. In fact, all financial matters fall within this house. It is also the house of birth and death, or alternatively beginnings and endings. Deep relationships, including those of a sexual nature, are dealt with, as are matters of the occult and the afterlife.

The ninth house

The ninth house, the house of Sagittarius and Jupiter, is from the opposite of the third, which is concerned with neighbours and matters local. The ninth focuses upon travel to foreign countries and extensive study, and also has been called the house of dreams. Longer-distance communication and matters such as the law and literature are covered by the ninth house. Indeed, all factors that potentially may increase one's experience or awareness are appropriate.

The tenth house

The tenth house is the opposite of the fourth house and looks outward to life in general, being concerned with hopes and ambitions and making one's way in life. It used to be called the house of the carer and the father, when perspectives and opportunities were more limited than today. As such this is the province of the long-term carer and also denotes responsibility in the context of the delegation, both giving and receiving. This house is pertinent when career changes are considered, and is associated with Capricorn and Saturn.

The eleventh house

The eleventh house is associated with Aquarius and Uranus. It is the house of acquaintances, social contacts and friends (but not close friends), and as such may encompass societies, clubs and similar groupings. It also provides an indication of whether a person looks favourably upon charitable causes and whether any activities in this direction are genuine or for the self – the house of social conscience in effect. It was called the house of hopes and wishes.

The twelfth house

The twelfth house, associated with Pisces and Neptune, is linked with things that are hidden, self-sacrifice, psychic matters and also matters of an institutional nature. This last aspect may refer to hospitals or prisons, and as such may include the more serious illnesses. It can also shed light on problems of a psychological nature, reflected to some extent in its previous name – the house of sorrows.

The following section on the Sun signs, provides more information on personality, characteristics, associations and aspects of personal involvement and interaction.

The Sun signs

sign: ARIES ♈

dates: 21 March to 20 April

origin and glyph: the ram's horns, which may be traced back to Egypt.

ruling planet and groupings: Mars; masculine, cardinal and fire.

typical traits: Arians have several noticeable characteristics, such as courage, seemingly boundless energy, enthusiasm, initiative and enterprise, and a desire for adventure and travel. This means that when faced with a particular challenge, there is a tendency to rush in without heeding the consequences, and this can often cause problems. This impulsiveness is, of course, one of their less appealing traits, and it may also be accompanied by selfishness. This manifests itself in the need to accomplish set tasks and reach planned goals, although they tend to have the beneficial quality of being able to concentrate on the primary aim by removing anything that is unnecessary and of little importance. Competitiveness is never far from the surface for an Arian, no matter what aspect of life is involved.

family: in personal relationships, Arians can be very passionate, and Aries men look for a strong partner. Arian women are equally demanding and often prefer a career to being at home, although the two can be combined. Providing there are no adverse influences elsewhere on a person's chart, Arians are faithful but there are those who are continually moving on to new relationships and challenges.

Children of this sign tend to show the typical traits of liveliness and enthusiasm, but because there is always an underlying impatience, a child may soon lose interest and be looking for something new. Performance at school may be chequered because of this trait. However, should such a child lose his or her place or standing, his or her natural competitiveness and wish to lead usually reassert themselves, and lost ground is regained and held.

As parents Arians are, not unexpectedly, energetic and in the main will encourage their children in a variety of activities. It is all too easy, however, for the ebullience of the parent to overshadow the wishes of the child, and that can easily result in discord.

business: to satisfy the Arian character, an occupation ought to be challenging, with goals to aim for and with the opportunity to lead. Boring, routine jobs would not satisfy, but if that were the outcome then other activities would have to compensate. Large organisations with some freedom and a defined career structure, such as teaching, the police or the civil service, would be appropriate.

wider aspects: in their other pursuits, Arians import their eager approach, which in certain circumstances can be positively damaging, for example, knocks and bruises in the early years.

associations: *colour* – red; *flowers* – thistle, honeysuckle; *gemstone* – diamond; *trees* – thorn-bearing varieties; *food* – traditional rather than exotic.

sign: TAURUS ♉

dates: 21 April to 21 May

origin and glyph: the bull's head, which has links with early civilisations in Egypt.

ruling planet and groupings: Venus; feminine, fixed and earth.

typical traits: Taureans rely upon stability and security, both in an emotional and financial context, but granted this they can be extremely reliable, patient and tenacious. They tend to be persistent, methodical and see things through to the end, and this can be reflected in their steady progress through life, including their career. Their lack of flexibility can often lead to resistance to change, even when it is for the better. However, when facing the challenge, they usually cope better than most. Taureans are practical people who dislike waste, and they tend to have high standards.

family: a good partnership is important to Taureans, and this means a happy harmonious partnership. Their need to put down roots and build can render them very good at making a home, as does the practical side of their character. They usually make good husbands and wives, and parents, but they may make the mistake of getting stuck in a rut. One of the faults of Taureans is jealousy and possessiveness, which can often be applied to a partner.

Having established a good home, Taureans will probably consider children to be very important, and the parents will strive to make their children happy. Babies and toddlers can be slow to reach the obvious milestones such as walking, but in later childhood things need to be learnt only once. Discipline is important because Taureans are essentially traditional and look for rules and guidance.

business: although Taureans do not like taking risks, they are ambitious. However, they are more likely to stay with a job than to chop and change, and will quite possibly remain in uninteresting employment because the income is well nigh guaranteed. Sure handling of money and financial affairs comes easily to Taureans, and many find careers in the financial sector.

wider aspects: routine is vital, and change or uncertainty makes them uncomfortable. They enjoy leisure pursuits but must guard against becoming too lazy.

associations: *colour* – pale shades, especially blue, pink and green; *flowers* – rose, poppy and foxglove; *gemstone* – emerald; *trees* – apple, pear, ash; *food* – generally like their food.

sign: GEMINI ♊

dates: 22 May to 21 June

origin and glyph: two children, from Castor and Pollux of Classical mythology, which are bright stars.

ruling planet and groupings: Mercury; masculine, mutable and air.

typical traits: these include such characteristics as liveliness, versatility and intelligence, but these are tempered to some degree by a nervous energy and a certain inconsistency at times. They are logical, ordered and very quick of mind, seeking variety in their lives, both at home and in their work. They tend to be good communicators but at times let their desire to communicate dominate all else. They can take in information very quickly if they are concentrating enough, but run the risk of knowing a little about a lot rather than grasping one topic in great depth. This is not necessarily a bad thing, of course.

family: the Geminian curiosity and versatility render relationships a little more prone than most to disruption or diversion. However, partnerships can last, particularly if the husband/wife finds an interesting companion with whom he or she can interact intellectually. Gemini women often marry men who can deal with domestic chores, as such women have no love of housework.

As parents, they can be lively and creative but sometimes over-critical. It is not uncommon for Geminians to make poor parents because they can be too impatient, too heavily involved in their own careers and over-competitive, seeking reflected glory in their children's achievements.

Gemini children are likely to talk and walk relatively early, and it will be necessary to keep them well occupied. It is often advisable to encourage them to finish anything they have started, to ensure numerous tasks are not left in various stages of completion. Because Geminians can also be quite cunning, and although they may be very able at school, they can often put their own thoughts before hard facts.

business: Geminians are very good when dealing with money and can, therefore, be admirably suited to banking or accountancy. As might be expected, the ability to communicate and the lively personality mean they may also fit well into employment in some aspect of the media or advertising. The pitfalls inevitably are that attention to detail may be lacking and that there must be variety. Conversely, they handle pressure well and are good at handling several tasks at once.

wider aspects: change and variety remain of paramount importance, whether in leisure pursuits or retirement. Individualism will dominate over group activities, which may become routine.

associations: *colour* – yellow, although most are liked; *flowers* – lavender, lily of the valley; *gemstone* – agate; *trees* – any tree producing nuts; *food* – salads and fruit, fish.

sign: CANCER ♋

dates: 22 June to 22 July

origin and glyph: the glyph represents the breasts; Cancer probably came from ancient Babylon.

ruling planet and groupings: Moon; feminine, cardinal and water.

typical traits: the protective nature of the Cancerian is the overriding aspect of the character, but it is tempered by a stubborn and often moody streak. Although they tend to be of the worrying type, Cancerians have a remarkably good intuition, and their instinctive reactions and decisions can usually be relied upon. There is, however, a changeability about Cancerians that manifests itself in several ways. They can rapidly adapt to pick up information, habits, etc, from others. It also means that they can be touchy and, like the crab, may be hiding a soft, easily hurt person beneath a seemingly hard shell.

family: the caring nature of Cancerians makes them excellent at building a home and good at forming long-lasting partnerships. In general Cancerians like to look back in preference to forwards and commonly stay in the same house for a long period of time. A slightly negative aspect is that their protective nature can become excessive and turn into clinging, and they may be touchy and occasionally snap for no apparent reason.

The sensitive almost retiring aspect of the character can be seen quite early in life, and this may continue to the point that they become very shy at school; they may hide behind a shell. It is commonly the case that Cancerians will eye new social contacts somewhat warily, keeping them at arm's length. However, when they get to know each other better, firm friendships can develop.

Cancerians usually like their extended family within a reasonably short distance and are keen to help anyone who may need their support.

business: Cancerians can turn their hand to most things, and their careful, intuitive approach can make them successful. They tend to work well with people and often adopt the role of mediator, where diplomacy is required. The caring professions (for example, medicine) are obviously well matched to the Cancer character, but teaching may also be suitable. Although business may prosper under a Cancerian, there is often a tendency, even a fear, to change, which may show itself as inflexibility.

wider aspects: Cancerians are extremely sensitive, and while outwardly they appear charming and friendly, they can be temperamental and subject to wide mood swings. In general they love change, and while travel appeals, home has the greatest attraction.

associations: *colour* – silver and pastel shades; *flowers* – white flowers, especially the rose, lily; *gemstone* – pearl; *trees* – none in particular; *food* – dairy foods and fish.

sign: LEO ♌

dates: 23 July to 23 August

origin and glyph: it probably originated in ancient Egypt, from the constellation; the glyph resembles the lion's tail.

ruling planet and groupings: Sun; masculine, fixed, fire.

typical traits: Leonians tend to be generous, creative and yet proud individuals who nevertheless need to keep a tight rein on themselves to avoid becoming overbearing. The creative nature needs to find an outlet in whatever guise, and it is common for Leonians to become organisers, with confidence and energy, although beneath that they may be rather nervous. The possible risk is that Leonians may end up taking over and feel they always know best, so they must learn to listen to the views of other people. They can also display a temper, if only briefly, and are prone to panic if things go badly wrong. However, they generally regain control of the situation quickly. Their impatience and tendency to go over the top are countered by the abundance of their positive qualities.

family: to their partners Leonians will be affectionate, but their strong will and urge to lead can make them rather domineering. However, they can be very sensitive, and criticism can cut deeply. As parents, Leonians understand and encourage their children and will do anything to ensure they are not unhappy. However, they are not over-compliant and often associate with traditional values when it comes to behaviour and education.

Leo children tend to have an outgoing and bright personality, but they must not be allowed to be bossy towards other children, nor must their stubborn streak be allowed to develop.

However, any criticism must be levelled in such a way as not to dent the rather fragile Leo self-confidence.

business: whatever their occupation or position, Leo individuals will work hard, in part because they are happier when they have people working for them. For many, luxury or glamour will appeal, and if they can achieve this through their employment then so much the better. As such, they may turn to acting, sport or working in the jewellery trade. They will often go for highly paid jobs, which they equate with status, but, equally, they make good employers, expecting the best of their employees but generous in return.

wider aspects: the Leonian is better leading rather than following and excels where generalities rather than attention to detail are accepted.

associations: *colour* – gold and scarlet; *flowers* – marigold, sunflower; *gemstone* – ruby; *trees* – citrus, walnut, olive; *food* – honey and cereals, most meats and rice.

sign: VIRGO ♍

dates: 24 August to 22 September

origin and glyph: the Egyptian goddess of grain (Nidaba) was probably the origin, and in old pictures the Virgin is shown bearing an ear of corn and holding a child; the glyph is the female genitalia.

ruling planet and groupings: Mercury; feminine, mutable and earth.

typical traits: Virgoans are traditionally shy and modest, hard-working and practical and yet, perhaps, rather dull. They have a well-developed tendency to criticise both themselves and others, and often allow this to go too far. If a positive tenor is applied to Virgoan traits, it results in someone who works hard, is sensible and intelligent, and very good at detailed tasks.

Being essentially a worker, Virgoans are not interested in taking the lead but more in completing a task to the best of their ability. There is a likelihood that Virgoans will be worriers, and they often worry about nothing at all, which can be misconstrued or counterproductive. However, their own positive qualities are the best tools to deal with such problems.

family: Virgoans are very loyal in relationships and fond of their family, although this love may not manifest itself openly but rather in private. They may be self-effacing or even devalue themselves by feeling unworthy. A more common fault would be to over-criticise, but in the main they are caring, sound partners.

Children like to be kept occupied and at school will be neat, tidy and helpful. Their natural shyness may make them seem aloof, but if they can build up their self-confidence this will help them to keep worry at bay.

A great deal of time and attention will be paid to the home to keep it nice, but care should be exercised so that standards are not kept too high.

business: as already mentioned, Virgoans are not particularly ambitious and therefore are happier when supervised at work. If attention to detail is required then they are very capable and proficient in problem-solving or working in science or medicine. Although they like to be appreciated, they are happier working as a member of a team. They have an incisive style, useful in the media and the teaching profession.

wider aspects: there is a desire for purity, perfection and happiness, which, provided that their self-esteem is strong enough, is attainable through application of their own qualities.

associations: *colour* – grey, green, brown; *flowers* – bright small flowers, e.g. buttercup; *gemstone* – sardonyx (a white/brown banded variety of onyx); *trees* – nut producing varieties; *food* – root vegetables.

sign: LIBRA ♎

dates: 23 September to 23 October

origin and glyph: The element of the scales may have several origins, possibly from their use in weighing harvests; the glyph is similar to a yoke.

ruling planet and groupings: Venus; masculine, cardinal and air.

typical traits: Librans are true to their origin – they are always trying to achieve a balance, whether between views, negotiating parties, or in their own environment. In many instances, because they prefer not to take one side or the other, they sit in the middle, and this indecision can be their greatest fault. Turned to positive effect, by combining their desire to balance with their undoubted charm, Librans make fine 'diplomats' and can often settle an argument to everyone's satisfaction. They are also easy-going and like quiet surroundings at home or work, but although they may appear vulnerable, they are in fact quite tough and ensure that they follow their own plans.

family: in relationships with a partner, Librans can be complete romantics and regard this relationship as very important, so much so that even the Libran indecisiveness can be overcome for a time. They tend to fit well into the domestic scene, being quite capable of organising the household with their usual equable approach to all things, including money.

Librans make kind parents, although they must ensure that they are strong-willed and insist upon children doing as they are told. The Libran indecision might irritate some children, and every effort should be made to answer a child's queries. Children with this Sun sign tend to be charming and affable, and are often popular at school. Indecision and laziness should be identified and wherever possible overcome.

business: as mentioned, the tact and evenhandedness of Librans make them ideal as diplomats, in public relations, or any profession requiring these qualities. Their appreciation of art and beauty lends itself to a career in the arts or literature, and fashion, beauty and related professions are all possibilities for them. Although they like to work with other people, especially those of a like mind, they are sufficiently ambitious to reach for the top, although any isolation that this might produce would be unwelcome.

wider aspects: Librans work well anywhere where there are pleasant surroundings that are well ordered.

associations: *colour* – blues and pinks; *flowers* – bluebells, large roses; *gemstone* – sapphire; *trees* – ash, apple; *food* – cereals, most fruits and spices.

sign: SCORPIO ♏

dates: 24 October to 22 November

origin and glyph: the origin of the scorpion is unknown, although it appears in numerous guises in ancient history. The glyph symbolises a serpent's coil and is linked with the male genitalia.

ruling planet and groupings: Pluto; feminine, fixed and water.

typical traits: Scorpians can show rather a mix of behaviour and character, on the one hand being very determined and strong-willed, and on the other being obsessive, awkward and arrogant. Once committed to something, whether a person or an ideal, they will be very faithful, although they are susceptible to being melodramatic, and when emotions become involved logic suffers. They are usually energetic, wanting the most out of life, whether at work or play, and will not relinquish their goal easily. Although they are perfectly capable of sacrificing others, they do hold on to what is right and will exhibit a strong sense of fair play and reason.

family: the Scorpian's desire to stay with a relationship holds good for partnerships, although their energy may need to be channelled if it is not to prove disruptive. They prefer people who are equally strong-willed but, despite outward appearances, may themselves be weaker than they look. They are certainly prone to depression, from which they find it hard to emerge, and this may contribute to the apparent extremes in marriage – some are very good, others less so.

As parents they will do their utmost for their offspring, but they can push a little too much and should consciously develop a balanced approach to parenthood, allowing their children some freedom.

Some children are often very affectionate but equally prone to sudden tempers. They should be helped to talk over problems to avoid depressed silences, and their emotional energies should be diverted into productive occupations.

business: when running a business, a Scorpian will work to his or her very limit to help ensure success and, to a certain extent, they welcome challenges and problems. They can employ charm when necessary but can also be hard and demanding at times. They also like financial security and are willing to work for it. Scorpians are well suited to being in the medical profession or in a profession where analysis and research are required.

wider aspects: the character of a Scorpian is built up of a fine balance of attributes, which, in a positive sense, can yield a tremendous achiever but conversely may produce someone riven with jealousy.

associations: *colour* – deep red; *flowers* – dark red flowers such as geraniums; *gemstone* – opal; *trees* – thorn-bearing varieties; *food* – foods with strong flavours.

sign: SAGITTARIUS ♐

dates: 23 November to 21 December

origin and glyph: the origin is unknown, but the glyph, represents the arrow of the Centaur.

ruling planet and groupings: Jupiter, masculine, mutable and fire.

typical traits: Sagittarians are essentially gregarious, friendly and enthusiastic, with a desire to achieve all goals that are set. They are rarely beset by depression, but their inborn enthusiasm can sometimes take them too far, and they may take risks. Although they are versatile and intelligent, their desire to jump from the task in hand to the next may result in some tasks being unfinished. In excess, their good qualities can become a nuisance, leading to tactless, hurtful comments (without the intent to hurt) and jokes that go too far.

family: freedom is important to Sagittarians, so much so that it may inhibit long-term relationships. After settling down, however, they are good in the family context, and their enthusiasm can help lift boredom or depression. Sagittarians will enjoy a friendship or partnership more if they are given a loose rein to enable them to do what they want. Often their ultimate goal is not materialistic but more spiritual.

As parents, this approach to life means that they encourage their children to be outgoing, and this is fine providing a child is not nervous or shy. The natural enthusiasm of Sagittarian children should be guided to productive ends, and their instinctive dislike of rules should be dealt with diplomatically. There is considerable potential in the child who has a gentle guiding hand upon him or her.

business: Sagittarians are not interested primarily in material gain and because they are particularly interested in education and travel, that is where money may be spent. Work of a varied nature is preferred, but care should be taken to make sure details are not omitted in the race to move on to something new. There is a natural desire to help others, which may manifest itself in a career in teaching, counselling, lecturing, the Church, law, and publishing.

wider aspects: when both mind and body have a certain degree of freedom, Sagittarians are at their best and will then employ their versatility and intellectual strengths to the full.

associations: *colour* – purple, deep blue; *flowers* – carnations; *gemstone* – topaz; *trees* – oak, ash, and birch; *food* – good food is enjoyed but overindulgence should be avoided. Specifically currants and the onion family.

sign: CAPRICORN ♑

dates: 22 December to 20 January

origin and glyph: it may have originated with a mythical sea-goat from ancient Babylon. The glyph, is said to represent a goat's head and a fish's tail.

ruling planet and groupings: Saturn, feminine, cardinal and earth.

typical traits: it is said that there are two types of Capricornian, one of which has greater and higher hopes of life. In general, they are patient, practical and can be very shy, preferring to stay in the background – but, they are strong-willed and can stand up for themselves. Capricornians have a reputation for being mean, ambitious and rather hard people. A mean streak may often be directed at the self, and ambition, if tempered with realism and humour, can be positive. Usually the character is enhanced by other elements of the chart to produce a warmer personality.

family: Capricornians make good partners, although they may come late to marriage to ensure a career has been established and that the correct choice is being made. Once set up, they are likely to be happy and to provide well, if economically, for the family. This aspect of caring can extend well outside the immediate family, and although there may be a lack of confidence, a Capricorn subject will not allow him or herself to be pushed around.

As parents, they can be too strict. However, they encourage their children and will make sacrifices to assist their child's progress.

Capricorn children may be a little slow to develop but usually come into their own eventually. They are very loyal and benefit from a secure background, which offers discipline, but at the same time they should be helped to build up their self-confidence.

business: although they make very good back-room people, Capricornians can make good leaders and do well in their own businesses. Many have an affinity for scientific work and pay attention to detail. They work well with people, although they tend to have an isolationist attitude, taking advice only grudgingly. One might well find them in local government, finance, publishing, building or politics.

wider aspects: those with Capricorn as their Sun sign are generally happy alone in leisure pursuits and therefore enjoy music, reading, etc.

associations: *colour* – dark colours; *flowers* – pansy, ivy; *gemstone* – amethyst; *trees* – pine, willow; *food* – starchy foods, meat.

sign: AQUARIUS ♒

dates: 21 January to 18 February

origin and glyph: there are several links with the water carrier, and the glyph clearly resembles water waves, although the similarity to serpents has also been noticed.

ruling planet and groupings: Uranus; masculine, fixed and air.

typical traits: Aquarians are renowned for their independence and the fact that they like to operate according to their own rules. This can lead to them becoming very stubborn, but they can be inspiring because they do not easily lose hope. Aquarians are friendly, although they may not be totally reliable when circumstances become difficult, and highly creative in terms of ideas. However, they are not necessarily sufficiently practical to see through the ideas. Overall, they may be a little perverse or paradoxical, but beneath it all is a gregariousness and a real wish to help.

family: because of their independence, Aquarians may find it difficult to establish an emotional tie. However, providing they find the right type, who is not weak but capable and sensible, personal relationships can be very successful. They are usually totally faithful.

With children, they are supportive but may find it difficult to cope with emotional problems. Children may be a little unconventional, and some school environments may not be conducive to the full development of their potential. On the positive side, children will be originators, naturally friendly, and show the Aquarian traits of creativity and an affinity for science. The natural friendliness should not, however, be allowed to develop into a trust of anyone, particularly strangers.

business: not surprisingly, Aquarians like the freedom to do whatever they want, and they tend not to heed anyone who tries to boss them around. They are highly inventive and are generally good with any subject of a technical nature. They are also highly competent at practicalities. This makes for a considerable range of occupations, and Aquarians often turn their hand to science, communications, teaching, social work and general administration.

wider aspects: Aquarians are by their very nature a little out on a limb and unconventional, but their very positive qualities make this an interesting Sun sign.

associations: *colour* – electric blue; *flowers* – orchid; *gemstone* – aquamarine; *trees* – fruit trees; *food* – a light diet is best, including fruits.

sign: PISCES ♓

dates: 19 February to 20 March

origin and glyph: there are numerous links between the two fishes and various deities from history, including Jesus Christ. The glyph represents two fish, linked, but also refers to the physical and spiritual side of the person.

ruling planet and groupings: Neptune; feminine, mutable and water.

typical traits: the Piscean person is really quite sensitive but above all is a highly sympathetic and caring person who invariably puts other people first, especially the family. They have great intuition and are good at understanding the needs of other people and make very good, kind friends. Sometimes they can take their idealistic and self-effacing stance too far, resulting in an unwillingness to face decisions, and sometimes they will rely on other, stronger, characters to lead for them. They are usually always tactful but should beware that helping others and becoming involved emotionally is not always a good thing.

family: in partnerships, Pisceans can be a little difficult to cope with, but with the right partner will help to build a welcoming home. They like visitors and to visit others, and their self-sacrificing attitude means that they will usually go a little bit further to make people happy, or an occasion just right. It is important that their lack of strong will is not exploited by a stronger character.

Pisceans love children and make very good parents providing they are not too 'soft'. They do have an inner strength, and can be very tough and resourceful if the occasion demands it and when they rise to the challenge. Children often take second place to others and may need some help with their self-confidence. However, they can be very good in science and with parental encouragement can be good achievers.

business: it is not surprising, with their caring instincts, that

Fate and Fortune

Pisceans make good teachers and members of the health and related professions. They tend not to be particularly ambitious but can have extremely good business minds. Success is usually more likely if they have a supportive business partner. Other professions that often attract Pisceans include acting, the ministry, and anything linked with the sea.

wider aspects: Pisceans have to be careful that in helping and caring for others they tend to ignore their own pursuits or problems.

associations: *colour* – sea green; *flowers* – water lily; *gemstone* – moonstone; *trees* – willow; *food* – excesses should be avoided, salad foods are very suitable.

The birth chart

All the foregoing is background information that helps in the interpretation of a birth chart or horoscope. A typical blank chart is shown below. The solid central line represents the horizon and the numbered segments are the houses, as described previously. On this chart are plotted the positions of the Sun, Moon and planets.

To begin with, the following information about the subject is required:

- the date of birth,
- the time of birth and whether it was British Summer Time or not, and
- the place of birth and the appropriate latitude and longitude.

From this information, the position of the ascendant and midheaven can be plotted, followed by the planets' positions. As each planet is placed on the chart there will be certain angular positions developed between them, and when these form spe-

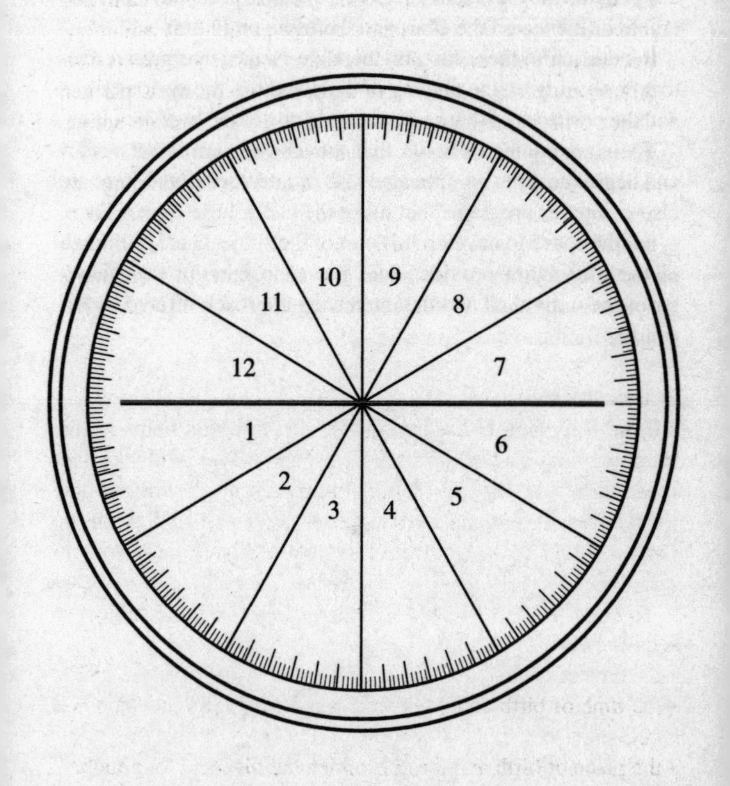

The birth chart

cific angles they are called *aspects*. These aspects have considerable influence on the chart and therefore on its subject.

In addition to these factors, there are further interpretive factors depending on the placing of the planets in the various signs and the positions of that same planet in one of the twelve houses.

There are numerous books that show how to construct a chart and begin the quite complicated task of interpretation. There are also computer programs that make the task a little easier. There is not the space to develop this part of the subject here, although all the information provided does give an insight into the character of the individual and the interesting approach offered by astrology.

Clairvoyance and Crystal Gazing

Among the many methods of divination, the most popular is that of crystal gazing, said to be convenient, consistently reliable and quick and is perhaps less distressing to the clairvoyant than many other methods.

This mode of divination has been practised from very early times with the aid of a crystal globe, a pool of water, a mirror, or indeed any transparent object. Divinations by means of water, ink, and such substances are also known by the name of hydromancy. Crystal gazing could be a very simple or a very elaborate performance, according to the period in history in which it was practised, but in every case the object is to induce in the clairvoyant a form of hypnosis, so that he or she may see visions in the crystal. The 'crystal' most in favour among modern crystal gazers is a spherical or oval globe, about four inches in diameter, and preferably a genuine crystal; but as a crystal of this size and shape is necessarily expensive, a sphere of glass is frequently substituted, and with very good results. It must, however, be a perfect sphere or flawless oval, highly polished, and held in an ebony or boxwood stand.

Among the Hindus, a cup of treacle or a pool of ink served the same purpose.

Precious stones were very commonly used by crystallomancers

in the past, the favourite stone being the beryl in pale sea green or reddish tints.

By the ancients, crystallomancy was practised with a view to the invocation of spirits, and very elaborate preparations and ceremonials were considered necessary. The early practitioners had to be of pure life and religious disposition. For the few days immediately preceding the inspection of the crystal, the fortune-teller washed frequently, and was subject to strict religious discipline, with prayer and fasting.

The crystal, as well as the stand on which it rested, had to be inscribed with sacred characters, as had the floor of the room where the invocation was to take place. Then, and now, a quiet place is suggested for the purpose, where the clairvoyant is free from all distraction and disturbance.

As well as these states of solitude and cleanliness, there is the question of the mental attitude to be considered, and this is no less important than the material preparations. A perfect faith was considered to be an essential condition of success. If the clairvoyant was to be accompanied by one or two of his friends or observers they also had to conform to the same rules and be guided by the same principles.

The time of the invocation was chosen according to the position of the heavens of the various planets, all preparations having been made during the increase of the moon. All the instruments and accessories used in the performance – the sword, rod and compasses, the fire and the perfume to be burned on it, as well as the crystal itself – were consecrated prior to the actual ceremony taking place.

During the process of invocation, the clairvoyant faced the east and summoned from the crystal the spirit desired. Magic circles previously were drawn on the floor, and it was desirable that the crystallomancer remain within these for some little time after the spirit has been dismissed. It was thought to be essential that no part of the ceremonial be omitted, otherwise the event would be a failure.

Later, the view was developed that all such elaborate ceremonies were unnecessary, and that the *magnes microcosmi*, the magnetic principle in man, was in itself sufficient to achieve the desired object. In due course, though the ceremonial was not abolished, it became decidedly less imposing. If the person on whose behalf the divination was to be performed was not himself gifted with the clairvoyant faculty, he looked for a suitable medium, the best for the purpose being a young boy or girl, perfectly pure and innocent. Prayers and magical words were pronounced prior to the ceremony, and incense and perfumes were burned. Sometimes the child's forehead was anointed, and provided with suitable clothing for the impressive nature of the ceremony. Some writers mention a formula of prayers, known as *the Call*, which preceded the inspection of the crystal. Finally, it was handled over the medium. The first indication of the clairvoyant vision was the appearance of a mist or cloud in the crystal. This gradually cleared away, and the vision made its appearance.

Modern crystal gazing is carried on in much the same manner, though the preparations are simpler. The crystal is spherical and of the size of an orange; when in use it may be held between the gazer's finger and thumb, or, if the end is slightly flattened, placed on the table; alternatively it may be held in the palm of the hand against a background of black cloth. The operation may be more easily carried out in subdued light. A medium or clairvoyant person acts as the seer and if the divination be made for anyone else it is advisable that he or she be allowed to hold the crystal for a few minutes before it is passed into the hands of the clairvoyant.

The object of crystal gazing is, as has been said, the induction of an hypnotic state giving rise to hallucinations, the reflection of light in the crystal forming focal points for such hallucinations. The value of elaborate ceremonials and impressive rituals lies in their potency to affect the mind and imagination of the seer. So far, the mystery of the crystal vision is no mystery at all. But the remarkable frequency with which, according to reliable witnesses, visions seen in the crystal have tallied with events happening elsewhere at the same moment, or even with future events, is a fact for which science has not yet found an adequate explanation.

It has been suggested that if telepathy operates with greater freedom during the hypnotic state, so it may be also with the self-induced hypnosis of crystal gazing. And this, though it cannot be said to cover the entire ground, is perhaps, on the whole, the best explanation on offer. There are many well-attested cases where the crystal has been successfully used for the purpose of tracing criminals, or recovering lost or stolen property. The telepathic theory, however, will hardly apply to these instances where events have been witnessed in the crystal before their actual occurrence. Such mysteries as these must be left to the art of the psychical researcher to unravel.

Clairvoyance

Clairvoyance, originally a French word, means the ability to see clearly. The reason so few people possess this extraordinary psychic faculty, is because many human beings seem incredibly blind, deaf, and insensitive to anything beyond the ordinary emotions.

The power of prophecy and acute intuition is a sixth sense which most of us have in a slight degree which often remains dormant and uncultivated.

Clairvoyance has often been mistaken for superstition or wilfully imposed and cunning deceptions, and it is difficult for many people to believe that it is founded on science and truth.

It has stood firm through the ages in spite of the quackery of wizards, the paraphernalia of sorcerers (used to inspire fear and awe in the uninitiated), the sneers of those of material minds. All of us at some time or other have felt the control of that still small voice, potent and penetrating as conscience, which comes, unaccompanied by earthquake or fire, to instil us with awe, joy, extreme sadness, or warning at some critical juncture of our lives; often anticipating, with power greater than speech can convey, some event that concerns our wellbeing.

Why this power should be deemed more extraordinary or mysterious than the senses of sight, hearing, smell, and touch which, even to those thoroughly familiar with the anatomy of the human body, remain steeped in mystery, it is difficult to say.

Science teaches that a million delicate sounds escape the ear and brain, and as many minute exquisitely fashioned atoms escape the eye.

A magnifying glass reveals the marvellous structure of insects and microbes invisible to the naked eye, and it is only by means of a telescope that the beauty of the stars is discerned; in this way the developed power of clairvoyance can be called the magnifying lens of the soul.

It is perhaps because this lens is dull and misty that we fail to see.

The history of ages and a great deal of our most cherished literature prove its existence.

Many of the stories and prophecies of the Bible are founded on clairvoyance. People were simpler and more trusting then; for this reason it is said that visions and clear sight were granted to them.

Pilate's disregard of the warning conveyed in his wife's dream, affected the whole course of Christianity, and the Bible abounds with examples of the disasters that befell those who disobeyed the spiritual promptings sent to them.

Colour and character

Clairvoyance teaches that everybody has a distinctive colour, which conveys more of character and personality than any word or action. The shades of these colours vary according to temperament, and are as much concealed from untrained vision as the million tints composing the gold purple and green bands of the rainbow.

- Optimistic people give out a pale blue aura.
- Large minded progressive people have a pale green aura.
- Pessimistic worried people have an aura which is grey.
- Ill-health in mind or body gives a dark green aura.
- Kindly benevolent, humane people have a pink aura.
- The thinker and scholar will have an aura of deep blue.
- The degraded have a brown aura.
- The passionate and bad-tempered have an aura which is red.
- The ambitious will be surrounded by an orange aura.
- The lover of beauty in art has an aura which is yellow.

These colours, however, although providing the key to the character, are subject to constant changes. Our moods sway and change our thoughts according to the happenings that affect us.

For example, bereavement or anxiety has power to transform the blue aura of the optimistic temperament to grey, and this temporary change of colour studied alone may puzzle the clairvoyant, and lead to a false diagnosis of character.

In order to prevent this, the seer should request some article constantly worn by the inquirer to be made available; the older and shabbier it is the better. A glove, an everyday tie or a ring constantly worn are equally valuable by which to discriminate between the temporary and habitual aura peculiar to temperament.

For example, when a man's glove emits a pale blue aura, in contradiction to the grey of his own personality, the deduction is that he is naturally of a hopeful and cheerful tendency, but that some mental anxiety or bereavement causes the grey, deep or pale, according to the depth of emotion dominating him.

The reason for this difference of colours is that the glove is, as it were, saturated with the essence of his normal disposition, while the colour of his character has been changed by circumstances or environment.

People of erratic temperament possess an aura of many and constantly changing colours, but those whose calm never varies maintain only one.

A few people are aware of the tones of their aura, and are therefore keenly sensitive to the influence of their surroundings.

They will be quite miserable if the paper on their walls, or the materials of their clothes, clashes in colour with that of their character; while they are at their best and happiest surrounded by the tints that blend or contrast harmoniously.

The clairvoyant and the crystal

The clairvoyant will possess six key qualities:–

1. The power of magnetism.
2. Mental health and influence.
3. Physical health and cleanliness.
4. Moderation in food and drink.
5. The power of discerning the aura and interpreting its colours.
6. Freedom from all bad habits.

In advanced clairvoyance the use of the crystal for vision is designated by many seers as 'claptrap' thought to be a vulgar 'playing to the gallery.' It is known to be bad for the eyes to gaze at any shining article for too long a period, yet in clairvoyance there is no doubt that it aids the concentration of sight and thought.

By means of crystal gazing the seer creates and becomes subject to the influence of auto hypnosis – that is, the ability to become entranced which veils his or her own personality forming a link to the client.

The surface of the crystal gradually reflects images, and subconscious impressions conveyed by and vital to the individual whose past, present, and future are being revealed.

Sympathy and intuition merge the gazer's aura with the temperamental colouring of the client. The seer's magnetic force creates further powers, while the sixth sense is the nucleus about which these are bound.

No student of clairvoyance can be successful in discerning character and personal emanations of colour unless disciplined by simple rules which should govern his or her life.

The clairvoyant should be approached in the same way in which one visits a doctor or solicitor, and there must be no determined reserve to conceal thoughts and character in the mind.

Clairvoyance in a room full of people is extremely difficult – indeed impossible, unless the onlookers can keep perfectly quiet.

It is always better to be alone with the inquirer in a small room where traffic noises do not penetrate, provided only with the necessary furniture, kept clean and fresh, airy, and well lighted.

The crystal should never be touched by any one except the clairvoyant, and must be kept free from spots and smudges. A black silk handkerchief round its globe will be a help to divination by preventing the reflection of lights.

The processes that occur in crystal-gazing are thought transference and telepathy. A communication of ideas is set up between the prophet and client, and the mirror-like surface of the crystal is the medium by means of which innate thoughts are reflected.

As far as possible, the clairvoyant submerges his or her own personality in that of the inquirer, putting himself in his or her place. Profound silence brings about the sense of atmosphere and aura, and by these means, and an intent gazing into the crystal, visions originate.

The crystal is supposed to be the magic bridge which gulfs the chasm fixed between itself and the spiritual world. In the iron it contains are situated the collective and culminating forces.

Mists of white, green, blue, and violet tints are symbols of good fortune and happiness; black, yellow, and red are warnings of disaster.

When the mists disperse and gradually ascend to the surface, the clairvoyant may reply to any question in the affirmative; mists that descend to the bottom are negative signs.

Images that develop to the left of the clairvoyant are real; those on the right are purely symbolical.

Chanting and controlling the mind

Words repeated over and over again have a mysterious power of isolating the sixth sense from the rest. For example, the word AUM is extraordinarily symbolical. It stands for three influences:-

A = the objective.

U = the subjective.

M = the eternal.

These are the kingdoms in the heart of man.

The objective, being the natural surroundings of objects and events which we all can feel and see.

The subjective, being the realm of influences the degree of which is felt according to the perception and training of our spiritual forces; too often vague and illusive, because most of us ignore its existence.

The eternal world, being that state to which the subjective world, in its highest state of development, leads this word repeated, slowly and steadily at first, and then at great speed, to have a marvellous power to create as it were a vacuum between the spirit and body of the prophet.

The mind dwells on its meaning; the vibration of the different letters acts on the mind, and the gazer is carried by gentle stages to the very seat of his spiritual being.

It is when the seer attains this full development that large, clear, and deep perceptions of the client's character are granted, and it is possible to reveal facts concerning the client which in a normal state would be absolutely impossible

The sensation experienced is that of being plunged into space in which the senses of sight, hearing, and touch are transmuted to the brain and spirit.

The student will most probably be discouraged at first at an inability to produce this state, but it should be remembered that hard work and perseverance are the attributes which all must give to attain perfection in any learning, art, or science.

One destined to become a great mathematician often stumbles in childhood with despair over the first addition sum, and the most distinguished musician has to do battle with the rudiments of music.

So it is in clairvoyance. Seemingly insuperable difficulties surround the novice who has never learnt to recognise the value and power of the sixth sense. Patience, a tranquil, determined mind, and not a little courage, are necessary in this branch of science. Time and growth work wonders in the persistent mind, and it will be seen that the obstacles gradually move aside, the curtain is lifted, and the strenuous seeker reaches that mature vision which he has formerly imagined dimly, if at all.

It is a good plan for the novice to ponder on his or her own name, and, shut away from all distractions, repeat it again and again aloud. The seer will gradually feel a sense of deepest mystery, for in that name is concentrated the riddle of existence. The blending of spiritual and material kingdoms lies behind it, and the material slips rapidly into obscurity.

Only when the heart is pure and worthy will the vision be granted – the clouds of bitterness, envy, hatred, and malice, which generally hide the precious jewel from the light, and render brilliance impossible, are discarded.

Everyone knows how difficult it is to control the mind, and keep it from mean and uncharitable thoughts. It is more rebellious even than the body, and influences it for good or evil.

Before all else, the clairvoyant must learn to discipline and constrain his or her thoughts.

A humble outlook, a longing for purity and singleness of purpose are needed to bring about the most noble qualities, and here it is that proper treatment of the body is invaluable.

Simple diet, early rising, daily exercise, constant isolation, and cultivation of good habits create the orbit for the higher faculties. These are the elementary rudiments of clairvoyance, and, unless they are mastered, the clairvoyant, no matter how diligent and persevering he or she may be in study and labour, will not succeed.

Tea-leaf Fortunes

The secret of success in this art consists of concentration, which enables the seer, who has a mind empty of all outside matters, to seize at a glance the symbols thrown up in the teacups and to read them intelligently so that the subject, or person whose cup is being read, can understand.

The cup must be passed directly to the seer by the person who has drunk the tea. If the cup passes from hand to hand before it reaches the seer, the fortune will be confused and undefined, and most likely untrue.

It is also desirable that the subject should sit near the seer when the cup has been given up. But the cup ought to be turned over on to the saucer to allow for 'tears' to be drained off the leaves before it is handed to the seer. It is extraordinary how tears, or drops of tea, will stay in the cup, however long it has remained turned over on the saucer, if there is matter for grief in the fortune of the subject.

Some subjects turn the cup round three times and touch the edge of the saucer with the cup, 'wishing the wish of the heart' as they do so. But unless there is a clear or outstanding star near the top on the inner side of the teacup, no more is heard of this 'wish of the heart'. (Wishes properly belong to card-reading.)

The seer or reader picks up the turned-over cup from the saucer, which the subject hands over.

You (if 'you' are the seer) hold the cup in your right hand. Note that the handle of the teacup is the house or home of the subject or 'place'. For someone whose interest is entirely in business, the handle may stand for 'the office'; for an actress it may mean 'the theatre', for a doctor, 'the surgery'. But for the average man or woman you will do well to read it as 'the home'.

The near or inner side of the cup, as you hold it in your right hand, is 'the fortune', the things that are happening or are sure to happen.

On the outer or farther side we read thoughts, things that may come, that are likely or possible but that are now very much 'in the air', unfulfilled, uncertain. If you read the same person's cup tomorrow or in a week's time, there may be quite a different story to be read from the outer side of the cup.

Some seers read a month's time in the depths of the cup, dividing it into two and reading the immediate fortnight that is coming from the top half, and the third and fourth weeks from now in the lower half of the cup's side. Happenings of a month ahead are near the bottom of the side. The very top is today. The rim is now. Close to the rim is by first post tomorrow morning. A leaf or sprig sticking out on the rim, startling news, now. Any sign sticking out implies surprise, even shock.

Note that the leaves or sprigs of tea dust – any combination of symbols, in fact – that lie on the bottom of the cup stand for trouble, annoyance, anxiety, mishap, bad luck, misfortune. Even if it is a star, it is a wish or a 'glory' that will cause the subject more sorrow than joy. And drops, moisture, liquid, things that stand for 'tears' always cling to the bottom of the cup. Notice especially that whatever you read in the bottom of the cup is timed as *now*. This is all to the good. Your subject's cup may be quite clear at the bottom tomorrow!

Sometimes, especially if the seer is reading a person's cup for the first time, and more especially if they are meeting for the first time, the skilled reader will rule out all 'time' and will read from the cup a fortune that goes far ahead and may cover the whole life of the subject.

The most experienced reader of teacups cannot tell what it is that impels him or her to do this, but does know that he or she is actually and truly reading what is sure to come true, and feels, with the feeling that is stronger than all knowledge, that what is 'seen' must be said. This rare and inexplicable state of mind looks beyond all symbolism. Symbols are no longer there; for the seer is now really clairvoyant, seeing nothing, but 'telling' of what is surely in the veiled future.

The meaning of the symbols

All the signs explained here are to be read as important or negligible according to size and clearness. Signs that disappear almost as they are read are true things that are ceasing to matter.

animals horses and dogs are friends. A lion represents a powerful friend. A tiger is an unreliable rich man, not necessarily an enemy. Leopards and wolves are enemies. A cat or a cow is a deceitful woman. Monkeys are mischievous people, especially if they are grinning.

baby a sign that one may be expected. If a cradle is near it, all will be well.

birds if they are in flight, birds say that news is coming. A bird standing is not such a good sign. A bird standing on one leg indicates plans frustrated or things changed for the worse since news was received.

circles *see* RINGS.

crosses symbolise things earned. A large, well-made cross tells of painful ambition realised. A small or ill-made cross implies obstacles, with danger of losses. A cross beside a grave, a funeral. Near to a wreath of flowers, a death. Not 'near' if there are no tears in the bottom of the cup.

dots are news, but of things of the mind, scholarship, science. Dots set as a triangle denote a wish, a successful but not exactly a material one. Dots are 'fine' things, sometimes ideas. Dots set inside small circles are money through business or affairs.

faces these are described to the subject, saying whether they stand for men or women, old or young, sad or joyful people. The subject must identify them. Sometimes the subject's own face is formed clearly by dots. Notice its position and the signs near it. But the fact that it is there, means that the day or the time is important.

gardens represent flirtations.

hearts two hearts tell of an engagement. If there is a ring around them or near them, this denotes a happy marriage. A crown over the joined hearts is a very auspicious sign.

letters denote the arrival of something by post. A dot in the middle of a square or 'long square' letter, tells of money by post.

letters of the alphabet alphabet letters are often thrown up in the teacup with astonishing clarity. These do not always stand for the initials of a name; they may indicate a town. But two or three capital letters together are, as a rule, the initials of someone with whom the subject ought to get into communication.

Figures must be read in conjunction with the symbols that are near to it.

lines lines stand for distance. Two lines are journeys by train or car. A ship is a voyage. Cars, engines and such things stand for themselves, but notice how they are placed and where.

masses or **heaps** masses or heaps of tea leaves are prosperity. The larger or higher they are, the more money or good luck is indicated. But masses in the bottom of the cup indicate that there is much anxiety even concerning what should be unmitigated good.

rings if they are small, rings mean business offers; if large, a proposal of marriage. Rings are always something that involves a question or an offer. A circle with a letter near it says the offer will be made in writing.

A ring formed of dots denotes an offer that is not so definite. A half or a part circle, not fully closed, is an indefinite offer or a half-question thrown out as a 'feeler' or with some hesitation. The same rule applying to smallness or largeness applies to the complete ring. It denotes business if small and marriage if large.

sprigs stand for people. Tightly curled sprigs are men, and more loosely furled ones are women. When upstanding, these are straightforward people, although if there is any kind of a weapon pointed at them, or from them, the message is 'Beware'. Sprigs set across are people who have been vexed. Look at the nearby symbols to find out why. Sprigs set sideways are people who are not quite trustworthy. People are also represented by faces, initials and signs, which the subject must identify.

squares tell of safety from a feared danger or deliverance. With a half-moon, squares denote danger of drowning escaped. But squares say that the subject is, for the time being, 'taking one step forward and two steps backwards' and, at best, is merely 'marking time', even if the square is set in the clear of the cup's side.

stars indicate successes, desires fulfilled, 'glory' achieved and startling success. If they appear in the bottom, something in the nature of fatality accompanies the good happenings.

triangles symbolise prevention of ill or trouble avoided. Look at the symbols nearby to interpret these more fully.

Enough has been said to show how the teacups ought to be read. 'The way to do it, is to do it.' A last word to the would-be seer: Never hesitate to say what you see clearly in the cup you are reading.

If you are sincere (selfless) in the matter and the subject is intelligent and anxious to know things, what you say is sure to be true or to come true.

Dice and Good Luck

Dice have been used for many games of chance and fortune throughout history. From ancient Egypt and classical Greece to the Far East, numbered cubes made of wood, glass, ivory or metal with their sides inscribed from 1–6 were popular for games and as a means of consultation. It was found through their medium that future happenings and events could be predicted.

Test this ancient form of fortune-telling:

Draw a chalk ring on the table or tablecloth. Three new dice and a new cup or shaker box are needed. All three dice must be shaken in the box, with the box held in the left hand.

If you throw all the dice outside this ring, ask no more, and, above all, steer clear of quarrels! One or two of the dice falling outside the ring indicates the same warning in a milder form. But the thrower, in this case, may throw again.

The following are the common interpretations of the sum total of the numbers on the faces that fall uppermost:

one (that is one dice with one point and two with blanks) says 'Nothing doing!'

two slight trouble, and rather a lack of good news. Nothing to worry about.

three good. Seize the chance that comes *today.* Your wish will be fulfilled, or a pleasing or happy event will take place.

four a disappointment; but it will turn out to be for the best.

five news of a death, but no surprise about the news.

six a marriage, news of which will surprise if not distress the thrower. Also a sign of the loss of a portion of wealth.

seven an omen of good luck. All will go well in the matter about which you are now anxious.

eight disagreeable news through the post. 'Sit tight'. Better news will follow.

nine this is a good throw. It is a sign of good happenings but with some touch of scandal. Success in love or reconciliation of a quarrel or disagreement could also occur.

ten uncertainty, but nothing worse. 'Wait till the clouds roll by.'

eleven danger of loss of money through treachery. This also indicates the illness of someone close.

twelve someone seeks to involve you in an intrigue. Refuse to grant favours that are asked of you. There is danger of you being made a cat's paw. Do not act without seeking advice from a friend.

thirteen warns you that an enemy seeks your downfall. Throw again, and if the number is higher, he or she will not succeed.

fourteen long voyaging but not yet. Your travels will prove profitable but not easily. Always have hope. This is also an indication of a new friendship to come.

fifteen some domestic trouble. Examine whether there are people making mischief in your home. Sort it out!

sixteen you are going to be lucky in a matter of which you are not hopeful. Tell no one of your gains for a week after you know of them. Sixteen also warns you not to think too much about money. Other important things are being neglected by you. You will not want for money ever, but it will not supply the need of friendship.

seventeen indicates something very good indeed, unearned, unsought, even undeserved. You may well be thankful when this comes. Perhaps a suggestion or proposal from a stranger.

eighteen this is the very best throw of all. It tells of a high destiny, great luck and happiness. But beware of inconstancy when your luck is at its highest. 'The full cup needs a steady hand.'

Fortune Telling by Numbers

Many of us think of ourselves as having 'lucky numbers'. We attach significance to some numbers for personal reasons, for example, those that are associated with addresses, ages or dates of important events. Every time we buy a lottery ticket we hope that these are the lucky numbers that are going to change our lives. But, there is also a fun way of divining the numbers that could play a part in your fortune.

Numbers have a major part to play in our lives. They are everywhere! There are quite simple ways of identifying the special number that brings you luck on a certain day.

That a certain amount of character and fortune may be revealed by means of figures is a fact that can be tested for itself. The results achieved by this method of divination are truly astonishing, and can be very rewarding to the mathematician in the attempt to solve the riddle of human nature.

Certain groups of figures stand for different qualities. Those given in the table following are only a small portion of the whole, but they are sufficient for the beginner. Each letter of the alphabet has its accompanying digit, and each digit has its abstract condition:–

A	1	Passion, ambition, design
B	2	Destruction, death
C	3	Religion, destiny, the soul
D	4	Solidity, sagacity, power
E	5	The stars, happiness, graces, marriage
F	6	Perfect labour
G	7	Course of life, repose, liberty, success
H	8	Justice, preservation
I	9	Imperfection, grief, pain, expectation
J	600	Perfection
K	10	Success, reason, future happiness
L	20	Austerity, sadness
M	30	Fame, a wedding
N	40	Fetes, a wedding
O	50	Pardon, liberty
P	60	Widowhood
Q	70	Science, the graces
R	80	A cure
S	90	Blindness, error, affliction
T	100	Divine favour
U	200	Irresolution
V	700	Strength
W	1400	Perfection of strength
X	300	Safety, belief, philosophy
Y	400	Long and wearisome journey
Z	500	Holiness
	800	Empire
	900	War, combats, struggles

The first thing to ask is the name of the subject. He writes it on a slip of paper, and next to each letter its accompanying figure. Here is the name, Dick James Smith:–

D	4	J	600	S	90
I	9	A	1	M	30
C	3	M	30	I	9
K	10	E	5	T	100
		S	90	H	8

Now they are added separately:–

Dick = 26 James = 726 Smith = 237

Add the three totals together:–

Dick	26
James	726
Smith	237
	989

The interpretation:–

900	War, combats, struggles
80	A cure
9	Imperfection, grief, pain, expectation.

The deduction being that Dick James Smith is endowed with a quarrelsome, headstrong nature, optimism, and inefficient will-power, which are destined to cause him trouble, loss, and misery.

Should the total of the names reach beyond 1390, the first digit must be subtracted, for example as in the name, Johannah Christine Whiting:–

J	600	C	3	W	1400
O	50	H	8	H	8
H	8	R	80	I	9
A	1	I	9	T	100
N	40	S	90	I	9
N	40	T	100	N	40
A	1	I	9	G	7
H	8	N	40		
		E	5		
	748		344		1573

Total = 2665, take away the first figure, leaves 665.

600	Perfection
60	Widowhood.
5	The stars, happiness, graces, marriage.

The analysis showing that Johannah Christine Whiting's life will be a mixture of joy and sorrow, the latter borne by a courageous and tranquil spirit. Her integrity and attractiveness of character will, no doubt, bring her much love and friends.

If the fortune-teller has a good memory, the table of qualities can be memorised, and a great aid to this is to practise with it perhaps analysing an author, statesman, or friend.

The fortune-teller's own name should reveal the fundamental truths of this method, and the analysis of people from history will show the distinguishing traits that have made them famous. For example, take Florence Nightingale:–

F	6	N	40
L	20	I	9
O	50	G	7
R	80	H	8
E	5	T	100
N	40	I	9
C	3	N	40
E	5	G	7
		A	1
		L	20
		E	5
	209		246

Total = 455

400	Long and wearisome voyage
50	Pardon and liberty
5	The stars, happiness, graces.

The numbers of the alphabet

1	2	3	4	5	6	7	8	9
A	B	C	D	E	F	G	H	I
J	K	L	M	N	O	P	Q	R
S	T	U	V	W	X	Y	Z	

Now suppose your name is Gladys Templeton, write it downwards, like this:

G	7	T	2
L	3	E	5
A	1	M	4
D	4	P	7
Y	7	L	3
S	1	E	5
		T	2
		O	6
		N	5

Total = 62

You have added to each letter the number that stands for it. Their total value added together is 62. These two numbers add up to 8. You may bank on the importance of this 8, though there are some numerologists who would add to it certain mystic numbers which represent the day on which you make the calculation. The above is simple and it works out, strange to say, with striking results!

Finding your lucky number

Suppose you were born on the 16th June 1971:

Take the date of the month	=	16
Add the figures together (1 + 6)	=	7
June is the sixth month, so add		6
Add the year of your birth		1971
		1984

Add these figures together:–

(1 + 9 + 8 +4) = 22 and
22 (*ie.* 2 and 2) = 4

You will find that the figure 4 will turn out well for you; also any figures or any number in which it appears; or any of its multiples 8, 12, 16, as well as 49, 48, 94, 84; and especially 40, for the 0 intensifies any figure which it comes after.

Note that number 4 itself is not a very good number, although it will be favourable for you. People whose number is 4 suffer from 'temper' – their own, as well as that of other people! To live in a house that is Number 4, to get a bus or train or theatre ticket in which 4 appears, more especially if the whole adds up to 4 or to a multiple of 4 – this means happy travelling, auspicious enterprises. Wednesday being the fourth day of the week, will be lucky; April, the fourth month in the year also, especially if these be the day or the month of your birth.

But should you particularly dislike this number 4, it is up to you to change it. Some people add the day of the week's number to those given, Sunday being number 1, Monday number 2, and so on. This plan, if you adopt it, gives you a different number. You may work them both together, using one for business and the other for personal luck. But do not change entirely from 4, if this number is serving you well.

The Tarot

Introduction

The Tarot pack is a set of illustrated cards which may be used for predicting future events or for answering almost any kind of question put to it through someone familiar with its symbolism. As a divination technique, it offers possibilities not contained in any other system and it is the only predictive method that is possible for anyone to understand and use after only a few weeks of study and practice. As with all arts, only years of experience will bring full proficiency, but mastering the Tarot does not require the unleashing of dark, supernatural forces or the invoking of ghostly spirits, as many would think, but rather requires an openness to impressions coming from the unconscious mind. We all have this ability – it manifests itself in precognitive dreams, feelings of foreboding, good or bad impressions of people we meet – but we usually ignore these feelings, dismissing them as irrational. Tarot reading is a way of harnessing these intuitive feelings and using them for personal guidance.

History of the tarot

There is little agreement on when and where the Tarot originated. The earliest cards used in Europe bear some similarity to cards used much earlier in Egypt, India and China, but there is little evidence of a direct link. One theory suggests that gypsies brought the cards with them from the east, but while it is true that travelling people have used them for centuries in fortune-telling, it is unlikely that they invented them. Another theory is that the cards are named after the River Taro in the north of Italy and that the cards were invented in the area around there. For many centuries cards similar in design to those in use today could be found in wealthy European households. These cards were more likely to be for playing games than for purposes of divination, and their popularity rose and fell depending on the fashion of the day. When they were in vogue, draughtsmen and printers, unfamiliar with the Tarot, would rush out new sets of cards to satisfy demand. This inevitably led to the designs being altered as each new set had some small detail added or left out.

It was not until the eighteenth century that people started taking the Tarot more seriously. This was the Age of Enlightenment and there was a great deal of interest in the customs, religious beliefs and ideas of ancient civilisations. Antoine Court de Gébelin, an archaeologist and amateur occult scholar from the south of France, wrote a series of books on a diverse range of esoteric subjects and claimed that the Tarot had its origins in an ancient Egyptian text called *The Book of Thoth*. That de Gébelin's theories were so readily accepted can be attributed to the widespread passion for 'Egyptiana' at the time in European society. Hieroglyphic writing, years before the discovery of the Rosetta Stone, frustrated antiquarians, and it became fashionable to suggest that the apparently indecipherable symbols could provide answers to questions that had plagued mankind since the earliest times. De Gébelin followed this trend and made a connection between the Tarot and Egypt, which was popular but which had no basis in fact.

Nevertheless, many writers took up de Gébelin's theories and attempted to expand on them. But when the hieroglyphics were finally deciphered and it was discovered that there was little or no connection between them and the Tarot, those seeking a mystic source had to look elsewhere. Alphonse Louis Constant, writing as Eliphas Lévi, eventually came up with a connection to ancient Hebrew beliefs in two books published in 1855 and 1856. This featured the Jewish mystical system of the Cabbala, which linked letters of the Hebrew alphabet to numbers. He devised a new system of Tarot, which more correctly reflected his theories, but again no hard evidence was offered as to the origins of the cards.

Today we do not know much more than in de Gébelin or Lévi's time. There has been a great deal of speculation and many claims for the source of the Tarot – other writers have linked it with Sufi and Cabbalistic origins or found connections with Greek mythology and pre-Christian religions – but so little evidence to substantiate any claim has been forthcoming that it would appear that the true origins of the Tarot are forever going to remain a mystery.

Reading the cards

The Tarot pack most commonly used today is based on an Italian form known as the Venetian or Piedmontese Tarot which became the standard version in that country by the beginning of the sixteenth century. There are 78 cards in this pack, divided into two parts: the Major Arcana (22 cards) and the Minor Arcana (56 cards). 'Arcana' means secrets or mysteries.

The Major Arcana cards, also known as the Trump cards, display mysterious, esoteric imagery which appears to be have been influenced by pagan traditions. From pack to pack there may be differences in style, position of the figure, dress and other similar details, but there is a strong common symbolism and their interpretation remains more or less constant.

The Minor Arcana features 56 cards that are divided into four suits, each suit having ten Pip cards and four Court cards. This is a similar arrangement to a normal pack of playing cards, except for the Knight cards in each suit. The Tarot suits correspond to playing card suits but they have different names: Wands (also known as Batons or Rods) correspond to Clubs; Cups correspond to Hearts; Swords to Spades and Pentacles (also known as Coins or Discs) to Diamonds.

Selecting your cards

Before one can embark on a reading of the Tarot it is important that you are happy with the cards that you intend to use. Tarot convention decrees that effective readings can only be obtained if the reader uses cards which they feel comfortable and familiar with – using someone else's cards, therefore, is seriously frowned upon. This is because everyone has a different psychic energy and cards owned and used by one person will have a unique psychic identity impressed on them. Cards should also be wrapped in a piece of silk and kept in a wooden box when not in use. Again, this is so the cards do not become tainted by another person's psychic energy.

The importance of ritual

Although there are many who hold with elaborate rituals and ceremonies when preparing a reading, it is generally recognised that such customs are not absolutely necessary. Formality of some kind is important, however, for two reasons. Firstly, a reading requires that the unconscious mind be brought to the fore, and this can only be done in a state of relaxation and quiet. If the reader or the person receiving the reading is overexcited, restless or nervous, then the intuitive, hidden parts of the mind will not be adequately prepared. In order to achieve the right conditions, small rituals and routines are invaluable – shuffling the cards in a certain order, for example, or lighting incense and saying a small prayer – calm the mind and create a better atmosphere. Secondly, Tarot combines random or chance factors with elements that are rigid and fixed, and in order to make sense of these properties there needs to be a solid framework to work within.

Environment

A Tarot reading should not be considered a spectator sport. Distractions, such as people talking or laughing, can turn a reading into a farce. Although it may be difficult to refuse giving a reading at a party or among a group of friends, the best results are always obtained by two people in a quiet room where they are able to concentrate their minds fully.

Selecting a spread

If you have little or no previous experience of the Tarot it is important to begin with a spread that you are comfortable with and fully understand. In the following section the Celtic Cross Spread is explained. This is a fairly easy one to follow and many first time users of the Tarot find it very useful. Experience in handling the cards will build the necessary confidence to attempt more complex spreads, but it is always best to master one before tackling another.

Using a spread provides a framework that enables the reader to relate cards to specific areas of the enquirer's life. This means that each card in each position relates to a specific aspect of the enquirer's life. Often it may seem that a card has no relevance to the area indicated by its position in the spread. In such cases the general meaning of the card should be adapted to suit the position in which it appears in the spread. Thus a card that suggests difficulty in a relationship may, in a position where career matters are indicated, be taken as referring to difficulties in a working relationship.

Shuffling and cutting

Before shuffling the cards, it is often suggested that a Significator be selected. This is a card that represents the person seeking a reading or the situation about which the advice is being sought. If the Significator is to represent a person then it should be chosen by the similarities in hair and eye colouring between that person and the card. If the Significator is to represent a situation then it should be a card which broadly describes the situation. If you do decide to use a Significator then it should be removed from the deck before shuffling and placed face up on the table.

The cards should be well shuffled before beginning the reading. If you intend to use reverse meanings then half the cards should be turned around and well dispersed through the pack. It is important that once the reversed cards are shuffled in the pack by the reader that they are not reversed again or the reading given will be upside down. Once shuffled by the reader the cards should be handed to the person seeking the reading for them to shuffle. The cards should then be handed back to the reader – all the time both parties taking care not to turn the pack around.

Selecting the cards

There are two methods of selecting cards. One is for the reader to ask the other person to cut the deck twice using their left hand. Each time the top of the cut should be placed to the left of the bottom of the cut so that three piles are made. The three piles are then collected so that the cards originally on top go to the bottom. The reader then lays out the cards from the top of the pack in the chosen spread.

The second way is for the entire pack to be fanned out, face down across the table. The person seeking the reading should then select their cards, being careful to keep them in order. The first card should always remain on top of the pile of selected cards as this way it is easier to remember the order in which they were chosen.

Laying out the cards

Once the cards are selected they should be laid out face down in their correct positions in the spread. Only when they are all correctly laid out should they be turned over – when turning them over it should be from side to side, not from end to end, as doing this will reverse the meanings. When interpreting the spread, the cards should be regarded as upright or reversed from the reader's point of view.

Before looking at each card individually it is a good idea to take some time to get an overall picture of the spread. If there is a predominance of Court cards or of cards from one suit then this can be significant. If there are a lot of Cups, then relationships and matters of the heart will probably be a dominant theme in the reading. Wands indicate that careers or other enterprises are likely to be important, Swords suggest some form of conflict or struggle, and Pentacles indicate practical affairs. A lot of Court cards together can mean that factors outwith the enquirer's control will shape their destiny and that the actions of other people will have an important influence on their lives.

Looking at the spread as a whole also makes it easier to relate cards to each other. This is an aspect of reading the Tarot which improves with experience and it can often be simpler for a beginner to wait until the end of a reading to make summing up remarks. In some spreads there are very obvious connections when certain cards next to each other develop one theme. For example, three cards in a row may mean 'the way forward', and are therefore intended to be interpreted together. Other cards may modify the meaning of the cards next to them, and more time and thought is required when interpreting them. The ability to assess relationships between cards comes with experience and familiarity, however, and the beginner cannot be expected to see in a spread all the things a more experienced reader may see.

The Celtic Cross spread

The popular Celtic Cross Spread is most useful for obtaining an answer to a specific question. To begin, the reader selects a card to represent the person seeking the reading or which best describes the matter about which an enquiry is being made. This card is commonly called the Significator. If the Significator is to represent the enquirer then the card should be one which corresponds in some way to his or her personal description. A Knight should be chosen if the enquirer is a man aged over forty; a King should be chosen if the man is under that age; a Queen if it is a woman over forty; and a Page for a younger female.

The four Court cards in Wands represent very fair people, with blond or auburn hair, fair complexion and blue eyes. The Court cards in Cups signify people with light brown or dull fair hair and grey or blue eyes. Those in Swords stand for people having hazel or grey eyes, dark brown hair and dull complexion. Lastly the Court cards in Pentacles refer to persons with very dark brown or black hair, dark eyes and sallow complexions. These allocations are not absolutely rigid, however, and you should also be guided by the temperament of the enquirer; a dark person may be exceptionally outgoing and gregarious and would, therefore, be better represented by a Sword card than a Pentacle. On the other hand, a very fair subject who is quite easy-going and relaxed should be referred to by Cups rather than Wands.

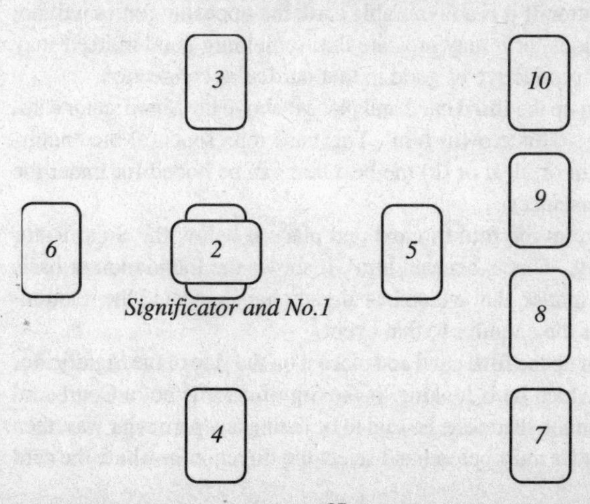

If it is decided that it is better to make the Significator refer to the matter being asked into then the card which is most closely associated with that area should be chosen. For example, if the question is to do with the success of a legal dispute, then the Justice card should be made the Significator.

Having selected the appropriate Significator, place it on the table, face upwards. Then shuffle and cut the rest of the pack in the normal Tarot manner, that is, three times, keeping the face of the cards downwards.

Turn up the top or **first card** of the pack and cover the Significator with it, saying, 'This covers him'. This card indicates the influence that is affecting the person or matter of the inquiry and gives an idea of the direction of the reading as a whole.

Turn up the **second card** and lay it across the first, saying, 'This crosses him'. This indicates the nature of the obstacles in the matter. If it is a favourable card, the opposing forces will not be serious, or it may indicate that something good in itself may not be productive of good in that particular connection.

Turn up the **third card** and place it above the Significator card, saying, 'This crowns him'. This card represents (a) the enquirer's aim or ideal or (b) the best that can be hoped for under the circumstances.

Turn up the **fourth card** and place it below the Significator and say, 'This is beneath him'. It shows the foundation or basis of the matter, that which has already happened and the relationship of the enquirer to that event.

Turn up the **fifth card** and place it on the side of the Significator from which he is looking. If the Significator is not a Court card and cannot, therefore, be said to be facing any particular way, then the reader must beforehand select the direction in which the card is said to be looking. Placing the card, say, 'This is beside him'. This indicates an influence which has passed or is passing away.

Turn up the **sixth card** and place it on the side that the Significator is facing and say, 'This is before him'. It shows an influence that is coming into action and will operate in the near future.

The cards are now disposed in the form of a cross, the Significator – covered by the first card – being in the centre.

The next four cards are turned up in succession and placed one above the other in a line on the right-hand side of the cross.

The first of these, or the **seventh card**, signifies the Significator – whether a person or a thing – and shows its position or attitude in the circumstances.

The **eighth card** signifies his house, that is, his environment and the tendencies at work therein which have an effect on the matter – for instance, his position in life, the influence of close friends, and so forth.

The **ninth card** gives his hopes or fears in the matter.

The **tenth card** is what will come, the final result, the culmination which is brought about by the influences shown by the other cards that have been shown in the reading.

It is on this card that the reader should concentrate all their intuitive faculties, taking into account all the divinatory meanings attached to it. In theory, this card should embody all else that has been gathered from the interpretations of the other cards.

The reading is now complete; but should the last card have not given up any conclusion then it might be worthwhile to repeat the operation, taking the tenth card as a Significator.

It is significant if in any reading the tenth card is a Court card. This indicates that the subject of the reading will be greatly influenced by the person represented by that card, and the outcome of anything troubling the enquirer may be dependent on his or her actions. If this is the case then more can be learned if the Court card is taken as the Significator in a fresh reading.

The Significator

1 What covers him.
2 What crosses him.
3 What crowns him.
4 What is beneath him.
5 What is behind him.
6 What is before him.
7 Himself.
8 His house.
9 His hopes or fears.
10 What will come.

The Major Arcana

The Trumps

The twenty-two cards of the Major Arcana, also known as the Trump cards, signify underlying influences on one's life. These are circumstances which are out of human control and are more commonly referred to as fate or destiny. They also represent things which are not apparent in day-to-day life but which are hidden from view in the subconscious.

Many experts also see in the Major Arcana the journey of life, from the innocence and wonder of childhood, through tests and hardships to maturity, and then on to old age, death and spiritual transcendence. The cards reflect such a path in life by using universal symbolism. For example, the Empress and the Emperor as the protective mother and the guiding father respectively.

The Fool

This card shows an attractive young man in a carefree pose standing at the edge of a precipice. He often has his belongings on a stick over his shoulder and a dog by his side.

The Fool represents a carefree, relaxed and open attitude. It suggests the ability to live day by day without worrying about the future. The Fool also signifies childlike qualities such as trust and spontaneity.

Reversed Childishness and irresponsibility are indicated when the card appears reversed. It can therefore be taken as a warning to be more responsible and to have more thought for the consequences of one's actions.

The Magician

This card depicts a practitioner of the magical arts. A lemniscate, the symbol of infinity, is usually shown above his head.

One hand of the figure, gripping a wand, is pointing upwards to the heavens and the other is pointing down, signifying the drawing of power from a higher source and directing it towards practical, earthly matters. As well as signifying skill in directing energies, this card also indicates charm, articulacy and the ability to lead others.

Reversed The inability to turn thought into action is indicated here. This is due to poor leadership and communication skills and a lack of experience and confidence.

The High Priestess

The Priestess sits between two pillars that represent the pillars of Jerusalem, Boaz and Jakin. One is black, signifying the feminine characteristics of intuition and mystery, and the other white, representing the masculine principle of reason.

This card signifies guidance of a spiritual or moral nature which comes from unconscious sources – intuition, dreams and fantasies.

Reversed The card can suggest a lack of inner harmony resulting from the suppression of feelings and the failure to acknowledge unconscious guidance. In a man's spread this reversed card signifies negative feelings towards women or that feminine qualities in himself are being ignored.

The Empress

This card shows a woman, often pregnant, sitting in a rich, fertile environment.

Unlike the High Priestess, who is virginal, the Empress represents motherhood and fertility. She also signifies physical and spiritual security and contentment in domestic situations and personal relationships. The benefits of this are generosity, kindness and the enjoyment of other people's company.

Reversed The Empress can also mean dissatisfaction with personal circumstances and a lack of material and emotional comfort. There could also be difficulties with physical health, particularly related to pregnancy and childbirth.

The Emperor

In contrast to the Empress, the Emperor sits in a hard and cold environment with a stern expression on his face.

This card represents masculine power and fatherly responsibility. In a reading it may indicate a connection to a position or figure of authority and could suggest that there is an opportunity to take control over others.

Reversed This indicates a problem connected with control, perhaps a dispute with a father or domineering husband or some other difficulty in a personal relationship. It also indicates a hostile attitude to authority and governance which may be nurturing resentment and rebellion.

The Hierophant

A Hierophant was an initiating priest in ancient Greece. He is depicted as giving advice to two figures in the foreground under his authority.

Originally this card signified the seeking of religious guidance, but in this secular age it represents all forms of guidance where the person giving advice is in a position of authority. Such authority figures include doctors, lawyers, professional counsellors, teachers and tutors. The card indicates that the advice given from such sources will be reliable and useful.

Reversed This indicates that advice given may not be reliable or that the nature of the problem is such that the advice is inappropriate.

The Lovers

Adam and Eve in the Garden of Eden are shown in this card with an angel looking down on them.

This card is not so much about love itself as about decision-making and commitment. The two lovers have their hands open and this signifies that the right decision will be made if there is careful thought and consultation. This applies to any major decision, such as getting married, moving house or changing job.

Reversed This is a warning against making a hasty decision or not making a decision at all and letting important issues go unresolved.

The Chariot

This card shows an upright warrior figure in a chariot with two sphinxes, one black, one white, in the foreground.

The rider represents self-determination and control. The sphinxes represent the opposing forces within human nature which have to be mastered before progress can be made. In a reading the card implies that with enough strength of purpose ambitions can be realised and obstacles overcome.

Reversed This is a warning against losing control and letting one of the two sphinxes gain dominance, thus pulling the rider off course. In order to regain control one has to be rational, assess the situation, and attempt to balance conflicting impulses.

Strength

This card shows a young woman taming a lion. She has a garland in her hair and around her waist.

The lion represents strong, negative emotions such as anger or jealousy and the woman moral strength and self-control. Together they show the importance of balance between these factors. A calm and rational approach in a situation where strong emotions may be aroused is urged.

Reversed Lack of self-belief, despair, and feelings of powerlessness are signified by the reversed card. These feelings can be overcome, however, if strong emotions are correctly channelled.

The Hermit

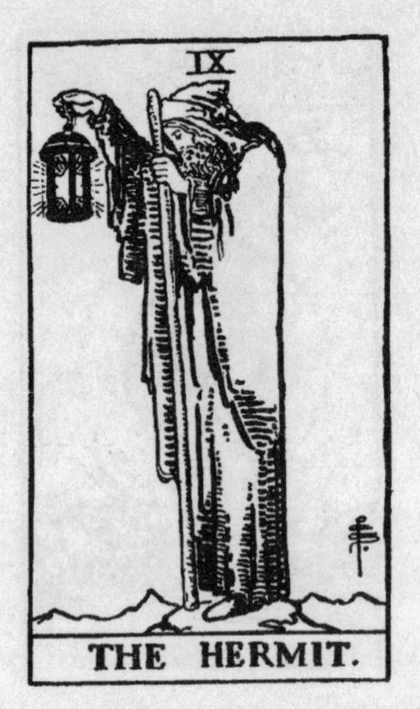

The Hermit is portrayed as an old man dressed in a habit and carrying a lantern. The barren background signifies isolation.

As the hermit has withdrawn from society, so the card signifies a need to withdraw and contemplate life. It also indicates a need to be more self-reliant and in control of events. This is especially true during times of worry or crisis. Help from others is unwelcome, however, as it is only through contemplation of one's own self that the strength to make progress can be found.

Reversed This indicates loneliness and self-pity. Instead of living in the past the card urges one to look forward and seek solutions to problems.

Wheel of Fortune

The Wheel of Fortune is shown being turned by a sphinx, the symbol of feminine wisdom. Various animals are shown around the wheel, representing the Living Creatures of Ezekiel.

This card indicates fate and events beyond human control.

In the upright position it indicates good luck or the optimistic outlook that things will work out for the best. This can also mean that one has a fatalistic outlook on life, leaving too much to chance and failing to make decisions.

Reversed Usually this indicates bad luck and events out of one's control. It can also signify that leaving things to chance will be damaging.

Justice

Justice is depicted as a woman on a throne with a sword in one hand and a set of scales in the other.

This card signifies a legal matter and concern that justice be done. If the card appears upright in a reading then reason and justice will prevail and the issue will be resolved fairly without recourse to heated, emotional argument.

Reversed In this position the card indicates unfairness, bias and injustice. It may also indicate that in a situation where there is deadlock a completely new approach is required in order to make progress.

The Hanged Man

Although the sight of a man hanging by one foot from a tree can be a little alarming, this card is not a bad omen.

The strange hanging figure represents self-sacrifice and dedication to a cause. Often those virtues are criticised and ridiculed by others who cannot see the end purpose. It can also mean a change in attitude or direction that is personally rewarding but misunderstood by others.

Reversed This signifies lack of purpose and apathy, often coming about through the misguided pursuit of illusory goals and the neglect of one's spiritual wellbeing. It is a call, therefore, to re-order one's priorities and pursue that which is truly rewarding.

Death

The skeleton on horseback is often seen as gruesome and frightening by those unfamiliar with the Tarot. Usually, however, this card signifies change rather than actual death, and the flag being carried aloft and the shining sun in the background are symbols of new life.

More specifically, the card indicates radical change and renewal with one phase of life ending and a new one beginning. With change there is also some grief for things that are lost, and this has to be faced up to and overcome.

Reversed This signifies resistance to change and fear of the future. It may be that changes made in one's life are more traumatic the more one holds on to the past.

Temperance

This card depicts a winged figure pouring liquid from one chalice to another. One foot is on land while the other is in water, symbolising equilibrium and balance in nature.

Temperance in a reading signifies good self-control and a balanced personality. It also suggests that balance and caution may be required in a situation, particularly if that situation involves arbitrating between two other parties.

Reversed Imbalance and uncertainty are indicated by this card. This brings unhappiness, mood swings and self-doubt, and in dealings with other people this emotional instability means inconsistency and clumsiness.

The Devil

A card that is often misinterpreted. The Devil figure does *not* mean evil, lust and demonic possession. Rather it signifies unpleasant emotions, which all of us experience from time to time, such as anger, frustration and bitterness.

The figures chained to the plinth symbolise being stuck in an uncomfortable situation. The card suggests that feelings of helplessness can be defeated, however, and that possibly there may be solutions to the situation that have not yet been explored.

Reversed This means much the same as the upright card, although it can also mean that a bad situation has been allowed to go unchallenged for too long.

The Tower

This card depicts a tower being destroyed by a thunderbolt and the inhabitants falling to earth. A crown is usually shown being blown off the top of the flaming tower.

This card represents an unexpected blow to the ego or pride, which at first can seem humiliating and damaging. In the long term, however, it proves to be a useful experience from which lessons can be learned. It can also mean a physical injury, which, again, is not as damaging as it first appears.

Reversed This signifies some misfortune which could have been avoided or which has been allowed to develop over a period of time. In a sense, therefore, the resultant injury is self-inflicted.

The Star

The Goddess of the Stars appears naked, pouring two jugs of water, one on the earth and one into a pool. The setting is serene and peaceful, and the sky is filled with one large star and seven smaller ones.

This card indicates peace, contentment and wellbeing. This can come after a period of turmoil and so represents a return to physical and spiritual health. New beginnings and fresh experiences may be ahead.

Reversed This indicates the opportunity for rest and repair, an opportunity that may not yet be realised. The reversed card, therefore, is a sign of hope and an encouragement to someone feeling anxiety or self-doubt.

The Moon

This card shows a dog and a wolf howling at a moon which has a female profile within. A path leads from the sea, between two dark towers, to the horizon. A lobster is seen emerging from the sea.

This card represents confusion and lack of direction. The lobster symbolises unconscious fears of failure and despair, and the dog and wolf represent aspects of our animal nature that may do us harm. The woman's face on the moon is associated with delusion and deception.

Reversed Morbid fantasising and feelings of utter despair may have become a serious problem – it is time to confide in a friend and seek support.

The Sun

This card depicts a small boy riding a white horse while the sun, with a masculine face, gazes down.

The Sun symbolises success, happiness and personal achievement. In a reading this card indicates the possession of energy, optimism and high ideals, and it bodes well for the eventual fulfilment of ambitions. There is also a sense given of enjoyment and fun in the pursuit of one's goals.

Reversed This indicates a gap between personal plans and ambitions and the present reality. More effort, planning and dedication are needed. At the same time it is important to guard against feelings of despondency.

Judgement

This card depicts the dead rising from their graves at the call of an angel's trumpet, in Biblical terms, the Day of Judgement.

This card signifies self-assessment. In the upright position it is a positive appraisal and there is an acceptance of the past and a sense of satisfaction and achievement. The future can therefore be faced openly and without fear.

Reversed The card still signifies change, except that when looking back there is regret and remorse and a feeling of dissatisfaction with the way things turned out. This self-condemnation is damaging and usually unwarranted. It is far better to accept what has happened and move on.

The World

This card features a dancing woman surrounded by a laurel wreath and an angel, a bull, an eagle and a lion in the four corners.

This card represents the successful completion of a project or the happy conclusion of a phase in life. As well as a sense of fulfilment and contentment, there is a much deeper, spiritual sense of self-awareness and understanding.

Reversed In this position the card indicates a circle of frustration and boredom. A new approach is needed to break free of the cycle. It can also signify delays to the completion of a project or phase in life which may be frustrating and holding back personal development.

The Minor Arcana

The fifty-six cards of the Minor Arcana consist of four suits: Wands, Cups, Swords and Pentacles. There are 40 numbered, or 'Pip' cards, and 16 Court cards. The four suits represent the elements: the suit of Wands is associated with fire, Cups with water, Swords with air, and Pentacles with earth. The meanings of each card relate to the qualities displayed by each of these elements.

The Pip Cards

Unlike the cards of the Major Arcana, which relate to spiritual matters, the Pip cards represent everyday circumstances and events and how people feel about them.

For ease of reference the cards have been grouped by their numerical values rather then by their suits. The significance of the numbers is outlined below:

The Aces

The Aces represent two things. As a whole, they signify singularity or the unity of several components; individually they represent the elements of fire (Wands), water (Cups), air (Swords) and earth (Pentacles).

The Twos

The Twos represent the relationship between two entities. This can be a personal relationship or the relationship between two loyalties, emotions or impulses.

The Threes

The Threes represent the concept of creation and symbolise the product that results from some form of union, for example, a child. They also represent the link between two opposing forces and are associated with fate and divinity.

The Fours

Four is the number of the material world, representing the four elements and the four dimensions. As it is strongly associated with nature and matter it indicates stability and order.

The Fives

The stability and order of four is disrupted by the addition of one to make five. It is the number of disorder and confusion and indicates the arrival of difficult times.

The Sixes

Six is the number of days in the Creation so it represents completion and fulfilment. It also indicates reward for efforts and justice.

The Sevens

Seven is considered to be a magical or lucky number and is associated with virtue and wisdom.

The Eights

As four and two are the most stable numbers, their multiplication to give eight means that number indicates success, progress and personal development.

The Nines

Nine is three times three, so it contains the creative force of that number tripled. It also indicates the final stages of creation and the reaping of rewards.

The Tens

Ten represents a new stage in development as well as being the number of completion. It can also be seen as 'just enough', where one more brings in destruction or decadence.

The Court Cards

The Court cards in the Minor Arcana usually consist of a Page, a Knight, a Queen and a King. These cards are generally thought to represent particular individuals and can be seen as the person having the reading, people known to them, or people they are going to meet.

Each kind of Court card represents a particular kind of person, and the suit they appear in indicates what distinctive personality traits they have:

The Pages

A Page represents a child, either a boy or a girl, or a young woman. All the Pages are associated with the earth element, signifying practical matters, organisation and planning.

The Knights

Usually depicted on horseback, the Knights represent youth, progress and energy. All the Knights correspond to the element of fire and the fiery spirit is present to some degree in all of them.

The Queens

The Queens represent mature women. If the person consulting the cards is female, however, it can often refer to them. The associated element is water, indicating gentleness and other traditionally feminine qualities.

The Kings

The Kings represent mature men. As with the Queens, if the person consulting the cards is male it can often refer to them. The element associated with Kings is air, which indicates authority, rationality, and other traditionally male qualities.

Ace of Wands

This card shows a hand appearing from a cloud, gripping a stout club.

It is a strongly masculine image indicating creativity, virility, enthusiasm, excitement, personal growth and ambition. It is a particularly promising card to receive if starting out on a new venture as it shows that the ability and creativity are there to make it a success.

Reversed A misdirection of energies is indicated, and there are feelings of frustration, weakness and apathy. However, some of the elements of the upright reading are still present, and things could be turned around with self-discipline and organisation.

Ace of Cups

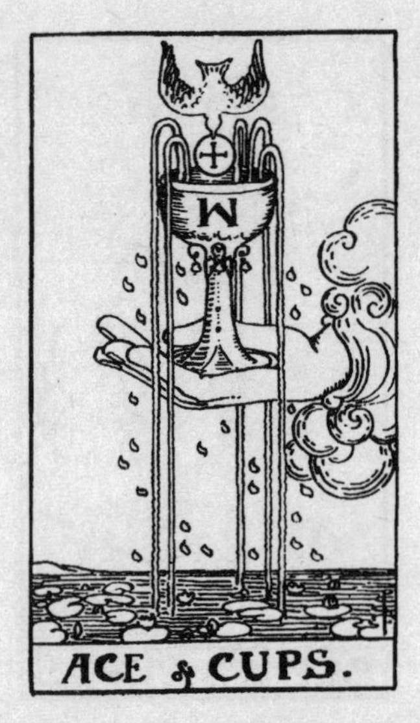

An open hand is shown in this card holding a chalice from which four streams of water are falling. There is also a dove descending to place a wafer in the chalice.

This card represents the feminine element of water and is associated with love, relationships and emotional growth. It shows that there is openness, contentment, and fulfilment in a relationship. Specifically, it could indicate a marriage or a pregnancy.

Reversed This indicates sadness and despondency. The water represents tears brought about by feelings of loneliness and a lack of security. There may also be an end to, or a disappointment within, a relationship.

Ace of Swords

This card shows a hand gripping a sword, the point of which is encircled by a crown.

This is a card of great forcefulness and represents the ability to think clearly and rationally. It also stands for justice and authority and can signify legal matters or some other dispute where clear thinking and decision making is required.

Specifically, it could mean that there is a sense of fulfilment when a correct decision has been made or when there has been a favourable outcome to some dispute.

Reversed This indicates feelings of frustration with what is felt to be an unfair decision or situation.

Ace of Pentacles

A hand from the clouds holds a pentacle in this card. Beneath there is a garden scene and a mountain can be seen through a gap in the hedge.

This card stands for fulfilment and stability in personal, physical, or material terms and a sense of total contentment with one's present situation.

Reversed This can indicate an unhealthy preoccupation with material gain, a poor home life, unstable relationships, bad health, or worry about financial matters. It may also show that for some reason there is a lack of enjoyment of life and an inability to see the good aspects of one's situation.

Two of Wands

A man is shown in this card with a globe in one hand and a staff in the other. He looks out to sea from a battlement which has a second staff fixed to it.

Wands are associated with careers, ambition and creative energy. This card indicates that some kind of crossroads has been reached and that a decision is called for. It suggests that this may be the time for assessment and planning.

Reversed This indicates some loss of momentum brought about by self-doubt and a feeling that personal achievements have not been as valuable as had previously been thought. There may also be a sense of anticlimax and a falling out with work colleagues.

Two of Cups

The couple shown in this card are pledging one another and above their chalices there is a lion's head supported by a pair of wings.

This card represents a love affair, a marriage, a business partnership, or a close friendship, and indicates that this relationship is of particular importance as there may be a need for support during a difficult time.

Reversed This represents problems in a once close relationship. This could mean an argument or conflict of some kind or it could mean distrust and a sense of betrayal. It also indicates that decisions regarding the long-term future of a relationship are best left for a time.

Two of Swords

In this card a blindfolded woman balances two very long swords on her shoulders.

This indicates that there is some sort of power struggle going on or the breakdown of a once close relationship and that there is a need for a balanced and rational approach to the problem. Self-restraint and caution against making rash decisions is indicated.

Reversed This card represents a tense situation which has become intolerable. Either one or both sides in the dispute are now venting their true feelings and there is little hope for reconciliation while both parties remain in this frame of mind.

Two of Pentacles

This card shows a young man dancing with a pentacle in each hand. The two pentacles are linked by an endless cord.

A balanced and progressive attitude towards the practical matters of everyday life is indicated here. Any problems which come up are easily dealt with and any setbacks which occur are soon forgotten. There is a general feeling of contentment and optimism.

Reversed A lack of balance is indicated and there is likely to be inconstancy and impatience in one's actions, mood swings, uncertainty, and periods of self-doubt which impede progress on many levels. There is also a recklessness and immaturity in some behaviour which is damaging.

Three of Wands

This card shows a male figure with his back turned standing between three staffs. He is looking out over a sea view and ships can be seen passing by.

Some form of creative initiative is indicated here. It may be related to a business venture, but it could also apply to a new career or lifestyle. Progress is very much dependent on luck, although there has been a good start made and there is every reason to be optimistic for the future.

Reversed This card indicates indecision, lack of confidence, and procrastination. No progress is being made and good opportunities which may not come again are being missed.

Three of Cups

Three cheerful young women are shown in this card lifting their chalices to each other. Around their feet lie different vegetables and fruits.

A creative force within the emotional realm is indicated as being very much to the fore by this card. This may signify a new relationship, a marriage, or the birth of a child. Alternatively, it could mean a period of spiritual, psychic, or artistic growth.

Reversed Intolerance and selfishness in a relationship are indicated by this card and a potentially good situation is being spoiled as a result. Divorce, domestic problems, argument and exploitation of another's goodwill are all indicated here.

Three of Swords

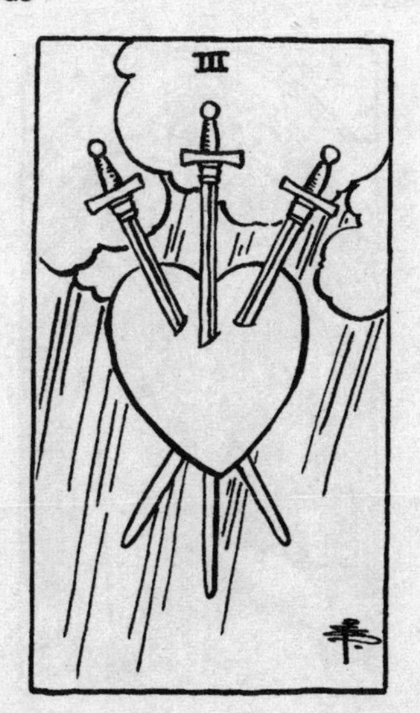

This card shows three swords piercing a heart. Storm clouds are gathered in the background.

Three may sometimes be an unfortunate number as it can mean conflict, aggression and the escalation of problems. There are also similarities with the Death card of the Major Arcana in that changes which may be good in the long term are very painful and difficult to face up to in the short term.

Reversed This indicates that a difficult and painful period of transition is likely to have lasted for a long time. This has led to conflict, argument and destructive practices being entered into out of a sense of frustration.

Three of Pentacles

A sculptor is shown at work here in a monastery while a monk and another hooded figure look on.

This card represents creativity, hard work and long-term rewards. There is a feeling that one's efforts and energies are being meaningfully employed and are helping other people. This is recognised and appreciated, which is also very satisfying.

Reversed This indicates that there is frustration because hard work and effort are not being recognised or rewarded as much as they should be. Often there is criticism and this further undermines confidence in personal ability and leaves a feeling of being taken for granted.

Four of Wands

In this card four staves hold aloft a garland. Two female figures stand in the background with nosegays in their hands and behind them is a castle and a bridge going over a moat.

Artistic expression and creative impulses being pursued in a calculated, methodical way in a stable and secure environment are indicated here. It can also indicate a rewarding holiday or a change in environment that bring new experiences and broaden the mind.

Reversed This indicates a situation where there are restrictions on creativity and self-expression in the form of rules and regulations. This is causing unhappiness and resentment.

Four of Cups

An unhappy young man sits beneath a tree in this card. He is contemplating three cups laid before him while a fourth is offered by a hand appearing from a cloud.

An underlying feeling of being in a rut is indicated, and there is little value placed in the good things one actually has. New experiences and situations are craved, which will stimulate and excite.

Reversed This indicates that boredom has become overly indulgent self-pity. It is possible that there are problems with reliance on alcohol, drugs or food. If so, then help must be sought to overcome the problem.

Four of Swords

This card shows a knight lying upon his tomb. Three swords are on the wall and one by his side.

This indicates a period of recovery from an illness or a period of contemplation after a difficult time, perhaps after a bereavement. It can also simply mean that it is time to 'get away from it all' and enjoy a well-earned holiday.

Reversed Feelings of being isolated and ignored are indicated by this card. This may result from illness or because friends have moved away or distanced themselves in some other way. It could also mean that a certain situation has been left behind but feelings of regret or resentment remain.

Four of Pentacles

This card shows a crowned figure gripping one pentacle and resting his feet on two more. A fourth pentacle rests on his crown.

A very solid domestic situation is indicated. There is great resistance to any form of change, which can be very good if it follows a period of hardship and struggle. It can also be very limiting, as after a time the situation may become too predictable and safe.

Reversed This is often said to be the miser's card, as it indicates a reluctance to give anything up. This can apply to a relationship, career, or any other aspect of life. A fear of failure is probably the root cause and this should be addressed.

Five of Wands

This card shows five youths playfully brandishing staves in mimic warfare.

Optimism and energy are indicated here. Little annoyances and minor setbacks are also indicated, but these should be regarded as interesting challenges to be met and overcome. This can actually be very satisfying for the enquirer, adding excitement to his or her life.

Reversed This indicates that the obstacles and setbacks are more serious in nature and that there is very little enjoyment to be had from them. There is also likely to be conflict and argument, possibly with one person who aims to disrupt another's plans.

Five of Cups

A dark, cloaked figure dominates this card. He is looking sideways at three prone cups. Two more cups stand upright behind him.

This card indicates unhappiness with the way some event has gone and a feeling of missed opportunity. Dwelling on what might have been is a futile exercise, however, and it is far better to accept things and move on.

Reversed The feelings of loss indicated by this card are more serious. It may be that someone or something very important has gone. This could mean an actual bereavement, in which case these feelings will persist until one comes to term with the loss.

Five of Swords

This card shows a young man with a disdainful look gathering swords. Two other figures are shown retreating from the field.

A sense of humiliation and defeat is indicated here. A personal weakness may have been revealed, or there may have been a conflict with a domineering person, which has resulted in exposure to ridicule. This is only a minor setback as it is probably only pride that has been hurt.

Reversed This indicates that more lasting damage has been done and that some form of betrayal, dishonesty or trickery has been involved. It may be that one person has been the cause of this upset, who is too powerful to be challenged.

Five of Pentacles

Two pathetic-looking figures, poorly dressed and apparently homeless, are shown on this card. Snow lies on the ground around them as they pass by a stained glass window.

Unemployment, financial difficulties, or the absence of love or security are indicated here. The problem may be alleviated, however, by the support of another party, perhaps a close friend.

Reversed This indicates an acute awareness of a bad situation. Poverty, domestic insecurity or unemployment may be signified, or there may be a general feeling of insecurity stemming from a lack of love or companionship. Things will only get worse if help is not sought to remedy the situation.

Six of Wands

This card shows a horseman with a staff in his hand which is adorned with a laurel crown. Footmen bearing staves are at his side.

Success and achievement in some enterprise is indicated here. A lot of energy and effort has probably been directed towards some end result and now that that commitment has paid off, it is time for celebrating and enjoying the fruits of one's labour.

Reversed This indicates that the completion of some project has been delayed or has gone without the proper recognition. Expected news may also have been delayed due to some misunderstanding or lack of proper communication.

Six of Cups

Two children are shown here, innocently playing in an old garden. They have filled six cups with flowers.

This is a card of the past and memories. It can indicate reward for past efforts and recognition for acts of kindness. It may also mean that reminiscing about the past will bring pleasure or that perhaps an old friend or lover will return unexpectedly to pay back a kindness or lend a hand in time of need.

Reversed This indicates being haunted by an unhappy past to the extent that the present cannot be fully enjoyed. It can also signify a reluctance to face up to changes in a relationship or in a domestic situation.

Six of Swords

This card shows a ferryman carrying passengers in his punt across calm waters.

Getting away from a bad situation is the theme of this card. This may be a slow and difficult process, and should be planned far in advance and adequately prepared for. It can also indicate a holiday or a move to a new job or home.

Reversed This indicates that a solution to some problem is only temporary and that a permanent solution has been avoided. Taking the easy way out may suffice in the short term, but eventually the problem will resurface and might be even more difficult to deal with.

Six of Pentacles

A well-dressed merchant is shown here weighing money in a pair of scales and distributing it to two beggars.

Fairness and balance with regard to money and possessions are indicated by this card. This may indicate charitable feelings and the need to 'put something back' into society. Generally, the enquirer is likely to be generous by nature and a person who gets pleasure from helping others.

Reversed This indicates a feeling of being taken for granted and not getting proper recognition. The situation may seem unfair, as if one person has been doing all the giving and another all the taking. It may also indicate theft of money or possessions.

Seven of Wands

This card shows a young man balanced on a craggy eminence brandishing a staff, apparently in self-defence.

This card signifies great personal ability, determination and energy. A test that calls for a supreme effort is indicated, perhaps an interview for a job or an examination of some sort. There is nothing to indicate failure, and there will probably be satisfaction in being able to handle such a situation well.

Reversed A challenge may prove to be too much, although it is more likely through lack of confidence than of ability that they will fail. Self-doubt is holding back the true expression of ability and that needs to be addressed.

Seven of Cups

In this card a silhouetted figure contemplates seven strange visions that have appeared before him.

This card suggests that choices have to be made carefully with regard to future goals and ideals. There may be a tendency to fantasise about future achievements. Those that are unrealistic must be separated from those worth pursuing – a process that calls for rational analysis.

Reversed Confusion and uncertainty are indicated by this card. There may be too many choices and possibilities for an easy decision to be made. Deluding oneself with unrealistic and unattainable dreams and fantasies is also indicated.

Seven of Swords

This card shows a young man apparently in the act of stealing five swords. Two more swords remain in the ground and a camp is nearby.

The chance to use one's intelligence to deal with a problem in a clever and skilful way is indicated. There may be some tricky opposition to face, but with cunning and guile they will be defeated. An unorthodox and unusual approach will often pay off.

Reversed This card indicates a reluctance to take chances or make pre-emptive moves to solve a problem or break a deadlock. Timidity, conventionalism, and fear of ridicule and failure only serve to prolong difficulties however.

Seven of Pentacles

The young man in this card rests his head and looks intently at seven pentacles attached to a clump of greenery.

This card indicates that sustained effort will bring the results hoped for. There is also the suggestion that a stroke of luck will progress matters.

Reversed This indicates a feeling of despondency and an inclination to abandon a project which is not progressing. It may be that mistakes have been made along the way which have put the end hoped for in jeopardy and which cannot be rectified. It is probably best to accept defeat and move on to something new.

Eight of Wands

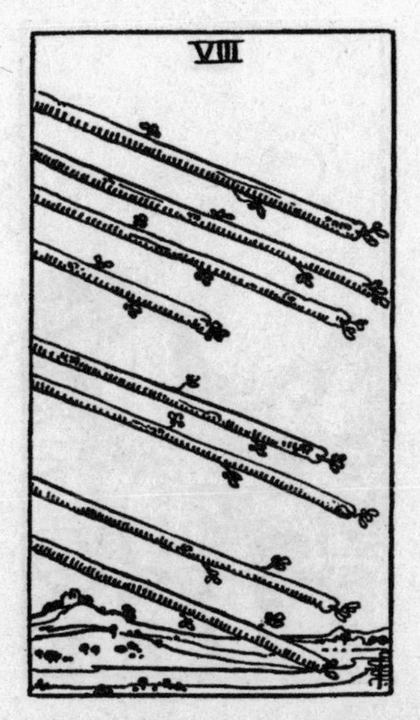

This card shows eight staffs in flight across open country.

Progress towards a satisfactory conclusion of any matter at hand is indicated here. There will be no more delays or hold-ups and things which have long been hoped for will start to happen.

Reversed This indicates that there is confusion and uncertainty as things are not going the way they are supposed to. Lack of organisation and planning, and an inability to cope with a complex situation, mean that although there is much activity and effort, little is actually achieved.

Eight of Cups

A dejected-looking man is shown in this card walking away from two rows of cups.

This card indicates that something very important is missing from one's life. There may be a good degree of emotional and material stability in the present situation, but a need to find a deeper level of contentment is constantly nagging. A drastic change in lifestyle may be called for to satisfy this longing.

Reversed This indicates uncertainty with future plans and a need to give things some serious thought. It may be that there is dissatisfaction with the present situation but very little idea of what one can do to change things.

Eight of Swords

This card portrays a young woman, bound and blindfolded, surrounded by upright swords.

A desire to make changes and improve certain aspects of one's life is indicated here.

For the time being, however, only small improvements are likely to succeed. This may be frustrating, but effort and perseverence will pay off in the future.

Reversed Feelings of being hemmed in and held back are stronger when the card is reversed. However, the situation is unlikely to get any worse, and if some small changes can be initiated now then later developments may be more kind.

Eight of Pentacles

This card shows a young stonemason at his work, the results of which he exhibits in the form of trophies.

Prosperity and personal satisfaction are indicated here, and there is a strong sense of achievement and pride derived from the exercise of one's own particular skills. This feeling may come from work well done or from some hobby or sporting achievement.

Reversed A problem with long-term goals and the frustration of personal ambitions are indicated here. Worries about money and short term security mean that too much time is spent on small and transitory gains that detract from working towards bigger goals.

Nine of Wands

This card shows a young man with an expectant look on his face leaning upon his staff. Eight other staffs are lined up behind him.

Rewards and benefits stemming from past deeds are indicated here. Hardships and struggles in the past, which have built resilience and character, are now being acknowledged. A more balanced, cautious and mature approach to life's problems has also developed.

Reversed This indicates a stubbornness and defensiveness stemming from bad experiences in the past. This undermines any attempt to progress with something new or different, and it is a problem that needs to be addressed.

Nine of Cups

A well-contented man resting after a feast is central in this card. Behind him, a counter holds nine cups, which are probably full of wine.

A general feeling of wellbeing and contentment in domestic affairs is indicated by this card. Generosity and unselfishness abound, and sharing this happiness with friends and family brings a great deal of satisfaction.

Reversed This card indicates complacency, false optimism, and poor judgement. Everything may not be as it seems – situations may not be as secure or friendships as close as assumed.

Nine of Swords

In this card a figure sits upright in bed, head in hands. Nine swords hover menacingly above the bed.

A preoccupation with past experiences, particularly those that were painful, is indicated here. There is anxiety about what other people think and say about you. There is also a fear of the future and an inability to relax, which may cause sleeplessness and depression.

Reversed This card indicates that the depression is more intense and persistent. There is also suspicion of other people being unfair or cruel. In such a situation help from others is required and may be the only way to improve matters.

Nine of Pentacles

A young woman is shown here standing among an abundance of grapevines. A bird rests on her wrist.

This card indicates that the pursuit of some goal has been successful and the fruits of one's labours can now be enjoyed. The pursuit may not have been easy, however, and this makes the final outcome all the more enjoyable. This card also indicates someone who lives alone and who enjoys his or her personal achievements in solitude.

Reversed This indicates insecurity and fear that achievements may be undermined by past deeds. It also suggests a dependency on another person and a sharing of the credit for some achievement.

Ten of Wands

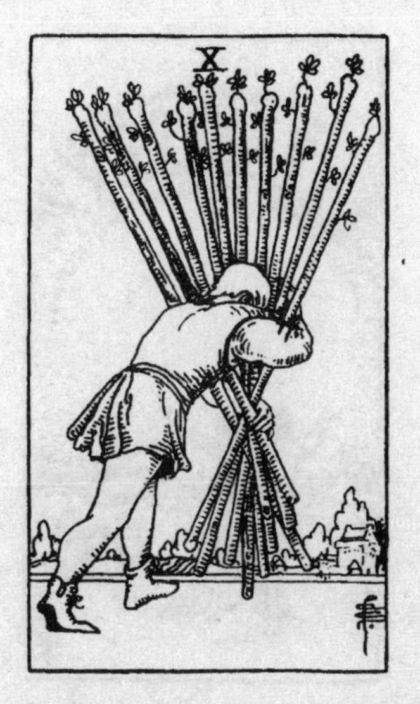

A man struggles to carry the ten staves held in his arms is shown here.

This card indicates overburdening with responsibilities and commitments. There is a sense of oppression, which is causing unhappiness and distress. It may be that pride is standing in the way of delegation, but if the workload is not shared then everything may prove to be too much.

Reversed This indicates that more may have been taken on than can be handled. This has led to tiredness, confusion and an increasing inefficiency. It is time to re-evaluate the situation and prioritise commitments, perhaps giving up some responsibilities.

Ten of Cups

This card shows a man and woman standing in awe of a rainbow, which holds the ten cups. Two children are playing happily by their side.

This card indicates fulfilment and contentment within the context of a family or group of close friends. There may also be the less favourable interpretation that one of the group or family is not as happy as the others.

Reversed This indicates that someone or something is disrupting an otherwise idyllic situation. If it is a person then it may not necessarily be his or her fault. It could be that the other members of the group or family are neglecting them and not paying attention to his or her needs.

Ten of Swords

A prostrate figure is shown here, pierced by all ten swords.

This card indicates that caution should be shown when getting involved in a new venture, especially if it means trusting people whom you don't know. It also signifies the conclusion of something that has caused a great deal of pain and suffering. In a business venture or relationship this may mean that the crisis point has been reached and that things can only improve.

Reversed This indicates that the crisis point has not yet been reached, so preparations should be made for further trouble. Again, caution should be shown when dealing with a group of people.

Ten of Pentacles

This card shows a man and woman standing under an archway with a child by their side. Two dogs are also seen in the foreground being petted by an old man.

This card stands for family support – in both an emotional and a financial sense. Everyone benefits from this system of support if everyone plays an equal role and gives as much as he or she takes. Financial benefits from family connections are also indicated, perhaps an inheritance.

Reversed This card indicates that family and friends may be more of a hindrance than a help, giving advice that has not been sought. There may also be problems with an inheritance.

Page of Wands

This card shows a confident, upright, young man surveying the land around him.

An energetic, lively, and resourceful personality is indicated. He or she is a good and reliable friend, and may also be the bearer of good news. This card indicates involvement in new and challenging ventures. A high level of enthusiasm and commitment is called for.

Reversed A self-centred personality with a tendency to gossip and spread hurtful rumours is indicated. He or she cannot be trusted with a secret. Bad news, or the delay of good news is indicated. Apathy and a lack of energy or ideas may also be signified.

Page of Cups

The young man in this card intently studies a fish rising from his chalice.

This card indicates an imaginative and studious personality with a good deal of charm and a natural modesty.

There are hidden talents which are now being discovered. Study and reflection are also indicated as being beneficial at this time.

Reversed A lazy, wasteful person lacking in direction and willpower is indicated.

Certain talents and skills are underutilised, and good opportunities for self-improvement may be being ignored or missed.

Page of Swords

This card shows a lively young man holding a sword in an upright position.

An intelligent and capable personality is indicated. He or she is thorough about things and may also at times be cautious and mistrustful.

Clear thinking and caution are called for. All proposals should be carefully considered before a decision is made.

Reversed This indicates a very cunning and manipulative person who uses other people and situations to advantage.

This indicates an environment of suspicion , which cannot be allowed to persist. A problem needs to be tackled head-on.

Page of Pentacles

The youthful figure in this card looks intently at the pentacle that hovers above his outstretched hands.

This card indicates a steady and dependable personality with qualities that can always be relied upon. He or she could be a student or an apprentice.

This card indicates a working environment with a fixed routine that is very boring. It may only be temporary.

Reversed A pompous and dull person is indicated who can frequently be obstructive and unhelpful.

This card indicates unhappiness and frustration caused by a tedious and dull job or lifestyle.

Knight of Wands

This card shows a confident young man astride a fast-moving horse.

This card indicates an attractive, adventurous personality, although there may be a tendency towards wild and unpredictable behaviour.

There may be involvement in new and challenging ventures. Holidays, adventures and lifestyle changes are likely.

Reversed A reckless, unreliable personality, always stirring up trouble and disrupting things. Also impatient, never finishing anything of worth. A difficult and stressful time is indicated. A disastrous holiday or an unwise career move may be signified.

Knight of Cups

A graceful young man on a well-controlled horse is shown in this card.

A sensitive and imaginative personality is indicated here. There may be a tendency, however, to indulge in fantasy rather than apply ideas practically.

Love, romance, and new relationships are indicated. There may also be opportunities for artistic expression.

Reversed This indicates a personality who is not as pleasant as he or she first appears and may have something to hide.

Indicates unforeseen difficulties in a seemingly favourable situation.

Knight of Swords

A determined young man rides into battle in this card.

This indicates an intelligent, courageous, loyal and trustworthy personality. He or she is very capable in demanding situations and makes a strong ally.

A period of some difficulty is indicated. The outcome will be favourable if a firm line is taken.

Reversed This indicates an aggressive, impatient personality, often in conflict with others, who wastes energies and creates problems.

In the difficult times ahead a hot-headed approach will only cause greater problems.

Knight of Pentacles

The young rider in this card sits astride a heavy horse and surveys what is ahead.

A practical and dependable personality is indicated. He or she will always work hard to get what is wanted.

The time has come to slow down and relax. Steady progress will still be made.

Reversed A very conservative, dull and plodding character is indicated who frequently displays great stubborness.

Little progress is being made towards what is desired and that the situation has become stagnant and boring. A change in approach is needed.

Queen of Wands

This card shows a confident, capable woman with an open outlook.

A sociable, active and resourceful woman who can direct her energies in several directions effectively is indicated. Outgoing and generous, she is a good wife and mother, and has many friends and interests. She will also have a good family life and be successful in business.

Reversed This card represents someone who thinks she is efficient and organised and who likes to be in control. This may be mistaken for arrogance, however, by those who resent her domineering and interfering attitude. She may think that others cannot manage without her.

Queen of Cups

The woman shown here appears rather self-absorbed as she contemplates a very elaborate chalice.

A quiet, reserved woman who keeps a lot concealed and so has an air of mystery about her is indicated. She is attractive and makes friends easily, but at times her personality may be hard to fathom. She is kind, intuitive and sympathetic, and her artistic and psychic skills are likely to be very highly developed.

Reversed This card indicates an impractical, frivolous woman, much given to self-deception and fantasising. She may be rather vain and self-interested, with few real friends to count on in times of need.

Queen of Swords

With a rather stern expression on her face, this woman raises her weapon in her right hand and rests the hilt on the arm of her throne.

This card represents an intelligent, independent and strong-willed person who may be very ambitious. Traditionally a widow, she can also be a woman living alone who is divorced or separated. Despite her strength and independence, however, there is a degree of loneliness and a need for companionship.

Reversed This indicates a very cold and domineering woman. Her hard exterior conceals an inner loneliness, however, and she uses her coldness as a form of self-defence.

Queen of Pentacles

This card shows a reflective woman sitting on a throne in a very fertile and nurturing environment.

A loving, sensuous, open-hearted woman who likes to create a good atmosphere around herself is indicated. She is a good wife and mother who enjoys her domestic security and likes to share what she has with others. She also appreciates beautiful things and loves nature and animals.

Reversed This card indicates a woman who is obsessed with material worth. She is often suspicious and jealous of others. Underneath the unpleasant exterior, however, there may be a very insecure person who craves love and attention.

King of Wands

This card shows an alert and capable man sitting on a throne decorated with lion motifs.

An intelligent, fair-minded man who is able to see other people's point of view is indicated here. He is good at giving advice and resolving disputes amicably. A considerate husband and father, he is generous to others, dependable and affectionate.

Reversed This represents an intolerant man who can be very narrow-minded and critical of others. He always believes that he knows best and is often accused of being patronising. He appears to be incapable of listening to anyone else's point of view and as a result is often accused of being insensitive and unsympathetic.

King of Cups

A figure sits on a throne surrounded by the sea. A dolphin is leaping out of the water on one side and a ship passes by on the other.

This card indicates a cultured, sophisticated, well-educated man. He may be rather difficult to fathom at times, but a cool and competent exterior could be hiding emotional difficulties. He may be afraid of intimacy and, although supportive of those close to him, be slow to demonstrate affection.

Reversed This card represents someone who cannot be trusted, especially in business. He may use his superior education and privileged social contacts to take advantage of others and deceive people who thought themselves friends.

King of Swords

This figure appears to be sitting in judgement. His sword is held aloft, and a stern expression suggests a cold efficiency.

A powerful, strong-willed man who is well suited to a position of authority is indicated. He is fiercely independent, does not like being constrained in any way, and enjoys trying out new ideas and innovations. His rationality and ambition take him to the top of his profession.

Reversed This represents a very unpleasant character who can be dangerous to know and is best avoided in all walks of life. He is intelligent and independent but also a bully, cruel and unkind to those around him and exploitative of those weaker than himself.

King of Pentacles

This card shows a relaxed and confident man sitting on his throne in a flourishing garden.

A good, honest, hard-working man who has achieved stability and security through his own efforts is indicated. He may be well off, but money has never been an important motive for his actions. His tastes are simple, and he enjoys the good things in life. He may be skilled with his hands and has a talent for solving practical problems.

Reversed This represents a weak person who pursues, but cannot find pleasure or satisfaction in, material things. He may take out his frustrations on other people.

Key Words

The Trumps

The Fool	*Upright*: innocence, trust, openness
	Reversed: recklessness, irresponsibility
The Magician	*Upright*: ability, confidence, communication
	Reversed: lack of ability, poor communication
The Empress	*Upright*: fulfilment, contentment, motherhood
	Reversed: insecurity, discomfort, hardship
The Emperor	*Upright*: authority, responsibility
	Reversed: inferiority, resentment, frustration
The Hierophant	*Upright*: advice, learning, teaching
	Reversed: misinformation, bad advice
The Lovers	*Upright*: commitment, decision, choice
	Reversed: procrastination, bad decision
The Chariot	*Upright*: empowerment, drive, ambition
	Reversed: conflict, misdirection
Justice	*Upright*: reason, fairness
	Reversed: injustice, bias, unfairness
The Hermit	*Upright*: solitariness, independence
	Reversed: exclusion, self-pity
Wheel of Fortune	*Upright*: chance, luck, optimism
	Reversed: misfortune, pessimism
Strength	*Upright*: inner balance, strength, control
	Reversed: helplessness, imbalance
The Hanged Man	*Upright*: perseverance, sacrifice
	Reversed: apathy, dissatisfaction
Death	*Upright*: change, renewal, rebirth
	Reversed: delay, indecision
Temperance	*Upright*: balance, caution, arbitration
	Reversed: clumsiness, uncertainty

Fate and Fortune

The Devil	*Upright*: anger, resentment, helplessness *Reversed*: suffering, despair
The Tower	*Upright*: misfortune, accident, humiliation *Reversed*: procrastination, self-injury
The Star	*Upright*: calm, healing, renewal, recovery *Reversed*: delay, prolongation
The Moon	*Upright*: confusion, turmoil, deception *Reversed*: fear, despair, helplessness
The Sun	*Upright*: optimism, ambition, success *Reversed*: impatience, frustration
Judgement	*Upright*: self-assessment, progression *Reversed*: regret, remorse, dissatisfaction
The World	*Upright*: completion, fulfilment *Reversed*: delay, frustration

Wands

Ace of Wands	*Upright*: creativity, energy, ambition *Reversed*: frustration, apathy
Two of Wands	*Upright*: assessment, planning, decision *Reversed*: self-doubt, anticlimax, conflict
Three of Wands	*Upright*: beginnings, optimism, luck *Reversed*: delay, indecision, procrastination
Four of Wands	*Upright*: creativity, openness, adventure *Reversed*: frustration, resentment
Five of Wands	*Upright*: challenge, growth, satisfaction *Reversed*: setbacks, conflict, argument
Six of Wands	*Upright*: good fortune, reward, satisfaction *Reversed*: delay, misunderstanding
Seven of Wands	*Upright*: effort, success, fulfilment *Reversed*: failure, self-doubt

Eight of Wands	*Upright*: progress, completion, fulfilment
	Reversed: confusion, misdirection
Nine of Wands	*Upright*: resilience, reward
	Reversed: reluctance, failure, conflict
Ten of Wands	*Upright*: responsibility, commitment
	Reversed: exhaustion, confusion
Page of Wands	*Upright*: energy, vigour, new beginnings
	Reversed: apathy, mistrust, suspicion
Knight of Wands	*Upright*: excitement, unpredictability
	Reversed: stress, impatience, recklessness
Queen of Wands	*Upright*: energy, ability, purpose
	Reversed: interference, arrogance
King of Wands	*Upright*: intelligence, generosity
	Reversed: intolerance, narrow-mindedness

Cups

Ace of Cups	*Upright*: love, emotion, growth
	Reversed: sadness, loneliness, disappointment
Two of Cups	*Upright*: support, trust, friendship
	Reversed: conflict, betrayal, separation
Three of Cups	*Upright*: optimism, growth
	Reversed: selfishness, exploitation
Four of Cups	*Upright*: boredom, apathy
	Reversed: self-pity, indulgence
Five of Cups	*Upright*: unhappiness, regret, loss
	Reversed: remorse, sadness
Six of Cups	*Upright*: reminiscing, rewards
	Reversed: nostalgia, delay
Seven of Cups	*Upright*: illusion, choice
	Reversed: delusion, fantasy

Fate and Fortune

Eight of Cups	*Upright*: development, sacrifice, growth
	Reversed: uncertainty, change
Nine of Cups	*Upright*: happiness, optimism, generosity
	Reversed: complacency, superficiality
Ten of Cups	*Upright*: fulfilment, contentment
	Reversed: disruption, unhappiness
Page of Cups	*Upright*: sensitivity, modesty
	Reversed: dissatisfaction, apathy
Knight of Cups	*Upright*: idealism, originality, optimism
	Reversed: deception, concealment
Queen of Cups	*Upright*: sensitivity, kindness
	Reversed: vanity, selfishness
King of Cups	*Upright*: sophistication, coldness
	Reversed: deception, manipulation

Swords

Ace of Swords	*Upright*: intellect, reason, fairness
	Reversed: injustice, bias, frustration
Two of Swords	*Upright*: argument, breakdown
	Reversed: conflict, aggression
Three of Swords	*Upright*: conflict, change
	Reversed: suffering, frustration
Four of Swords	*Upright*: recovery, renewal
	Reversed: isolation, loneliness
Five of Swords	*Upright*: humiliation, defeat
	Reversed: dishonesty, trickery
Six of Swords	*Upright*: renewal, rebirth
	Reversed: delay, postponement
Seven of Swords	*Upright*: intelligence, unorthodoxy
	Reversed: timidity, conservatism, fear

Eight of Swords	*Upright*: delay, obstruction
	Reversed: helplessness, frustration
Nine of Swords	*Upright*: anxiety, worry, suspicion
	Reversed: depression, isolation
Ten of Swords	*Upright*: caution, progress
	Reversed: conflict, difficulty
Page of Swords	*Upright*: caution, tact, wariness
	Reversed: mistrust, suspicion
Knight of Swords	*Upright*: courage, conviction, strength
	Reversed: aggression, impatience
Queen of Swords	*Upright*: independence, ambition
	Reversed: loneliness, coldness
King of Swords	*Upright*: authority, power, innovation
	Reversed: cruelty, exploitation

Pentacles

Ace of Pentacles	*Upright*: stability, security, contentment
	Reversed: instability, anxiety
Two of Pentacles	*Upright*: contentment, optimism
	Reversed: impatience, recklessness
Three of Pentacles	*Upright*: reward, satisfaction
	Reversed: frustration, criticism
Four of Pentacles	*Upright*: security, predictability
	Reversed: reluctance, resistance
Five of Pentacles	*Upright*: difficulty, insecurity
	Reversed: isolation, helplessness
Six of Pentacles	*Upright*: fairness, generosity
	Reversed: unhappiness, carelessness
Seven of Pentacles	*Upright*: perseverence, effort, luck
	Reversed: defeat, acceptance

Eight of Pentacles	*Upright*: progress, prosperity, pride *Reversed*: frustration, worry
Nine of Pentacles	*Upright*: achievement, security, solitude *Reversed*: insecurity, dependency
Ten of Pentacles	*Upright*: security, support *Reversed*: interference, hindrance
Page of Pentacles	*Upright*: dependability, security *Reversed*: frustration, unhappiness
Knight of Pentacles	*Upright*: practicality, dependability *Reversed*: stagnation, boredom
Queen of Pentacles	*Upright*: openness, sensitivity, generosity *Reversed*: materialism, insecurity
King of Pentacles	*Upright*: honesty, practicality, security *Reversed*: greed, weakness

Fortune Telling by the Cards

The qualities required to read the cards successfully are a good memory, a fine sense of the meaning of words, absolute sincerity and a wholehearted sympathy with the person whose cards you are reading (here called the subject).

A sense of the meaning of words is valuable in order to relate the cards properly. The good card-reader will not say 'very lucky' when she only means 'lucky'; nor will she say 'extremely dangerous' when 'very dangerous' is sufficiently emphatic.

Sincerity demands that the card-reader empty his or her mind of all thoughts, except those required to explain each card correctly and to relate its message with those of the cards around it, which will confirm or modify its meaning. Sincerity insists that the card-reader must be entirely selfless.

Sincerity and sympathy

Sympathy, which is love, ensures that the card-reader never tells anything that is bad except as a warning to the subject. Thus - 'avoid that person'; 'do not keep this engagement'; 'do not let yourself get entangled with these matters or with those people.'

Sincerity and sympathy are not incompatible. Cards can only tell what is known, although neither the subject nor the card-reader may actually be aware of it. Things are already sure to happen in the future because of something that has been said, done, or that has happened in the past; or because of something that is now happening though we may have no knowledge of it.

Note that the truth and usefulness of divination by cards depends on the intelligence, sincerity, and sympathy of the subject also. The subject who gives concentration, honesty, and love equal to that of the earnest card-reader, will be guided and helped.

The picture cards

Kings are men of weight – older men.
Queens are women and girls.
Jacks are young, unmarried men.

The suits

Spades stand for very dark people; Clubs for dark or brown-eyed people and Hearts for all who are neither fair nor dark – those with dark hair and blue or grey eyes, the chestnut-coloured people and the warm blondes, with eyes that range from the darkest blue to coldest agate grey. These are the largest class, the people called 'between colours'. Diamonds stand for the very fair, the 'lint-white' people, for the red-haired, and for those who are quite silvery white.

The subject must identify each Picture Card, after choosing 'herself' or 'himself' according to sex and colouring.

But these Picture Cards (or Court Cards) have additional meanings in certain combinations and under certain conditions.

It is only necessary, for the present, to realise that Spades represent trouble, anxieties, sorrows and changes that cannot be helped or hindered. Clubs mean success which has been earned or deserved. Hearts mean love, affection, company, socialising, and Diamonds stand for money, business and financial affairs in general.

Diamonds and Spades are 'chancy' suits; they stand for fated things, whether good or evil. Hearts represent things that can be altered by goodwill and sympathy. Clubs correspond to matters that, with some effort, may well be changed for the better.

The cards reversed

Some cards have a right way up and a reversed way. However, this is only the case with the Sevens and some odd numbers according to the way the centre 'pip' stands, and with all the cards when they are turned over if the design on the back has a 'right way up' and a 'reversed' way. Many designs are so ornate and intricately patterned that no difference can be seen, whichever way the cards come into your hand.

It is, therefore, wise to put 'R' on the top left hand corner of each card after turning the pack the wrong way up, if you can. (It depends on the design on the back; otherwise you devise your own 'reversed' way, excepting for the Sevens.)

The meaning of each card is considerably modified if and when it is, 'reversed.' In some cases it is altered entirely.

Some card-readers do not recognise different meanings in the cards when they are 'reversed.' But the seer who wants to tell of subtle shades of meanings will do so from the first.

The meaning of the cards

Diamonds

Ace Upright: A ring; paper money.
Reversed: A letter about money or containing money.

King Upright: A fair or white-haired man.
Reversed: A treacherous man.

Queen Upright: A fair girl or woman with white hair.
Reversed: A coquette, or flirt.

Jack Upright: A fair youth.
Reversed: A selfish relative, man or woman.

Ten Upright: Money.
Reversed: Journey concerning money.

Nine Upright: Sharp instruments; anger.
Reversed: Operation. With Spades; loss by death.

Eight Upright: Short journey; roadway; walk.
Reversed: Small money; a gain that will not last.

Seven Upright: Child or pet.
Reversed: Disappointing money.

Six Upright: Hope.
Reversed: Trouble with subordinates.

Five Upright: Gold, riches.
Reversed: The law; proceedings.

Four Upright: Society.
Reversed: Happiness.

Three Upright: Trade.
Reversed: Separation.

Two Upright: Fortune, sum of money.
Reversed: Surprise.

Hearts

Ace Upright: The House; between King and Queen, a love letter.
Reversed: Change of residence.

King Upright: A man 'between colours'.
Reversed: A fickle, inconstant man.

Queen Upright: A woman 'between colours'.
Reversed: A vengeful woman.

Jack Upright: A lover or one beloved.
Reversed: The best-beloved of consultant.

Ten Upright: Great affection; happiness; corrects bad cards.
Reversed: Change; birth.

Nine Upright: Success; desires fulfilled; the wish card:
Reversed: Love.

Eight Upright: Love and marriage; happy spending.
Reversed: Jealousy of men.

Seven Upright: Inconstancy; small success.
Reversed: Jealousy of women.

Six Upright: The past.
Reversed: The future.

Five Upright: Marriage.
Reversed: Arrival.

Four Upright: A messenger.
Reversed: Discontent.

Three Upright: Success; near Spades, insecure; near Diamonds, with money; near Hearts, with love; near Clubs, with ambition.
Reversed: Opposition to plans.

Two Upright: Love.
Reversed: Opposition to love.

Spades

Ace Upright: Business; high building.
Reversed: Death; annoyance.

King Upright: Very dark elderly man or a man handling important affairs.
Reversed: An enemy.

Queen Upright: A dark lady; a widow.
Reversed: Plots and scandal. With her Jack, a dangerous woman.

Jack Upright: A very dark young man.
Reversed: Night; shadow; medical matters.

Ten Upright: Distance; across water; voyages.
Reversed: Sickness; trouble. With Eight of Hearts; bereavement.

Nine Upright: Failure; loss; undoing.
Reversed: Death (corrected by good cards around it).

Eight Upright: Night; illness.
Reversed: Deceit; plots. Between King and Queen, a separation.

Seven Upright: Determination; change.
Reversed: Accident; upset. With Diamonds, most disappointing to present hopes.

Six Upright: A voyage.
Reversed: A surprise.

Five Upright: Mourning.
Reversed: A loss.

Four Upright: Solitude.
Reversed: A proposal.

Three Upright: A quarrel.
Reversed: Confusion.

Two Upright: A friend.
Reversed: An enemy, once a friend.

Clubs

Ace Upright: Letters; papers; good documents.
Reversed: Delayed letters; unpleasant news.

King Upright: A brown-eyed man; a good friend.
Reversed: Worried or perplexed man.

Queen Upright: A brown-eyed woman.
Reversed: A disappointed woman; sad.

Jack Upright: A dark-eyed young man.
Reversed: The thoughts of the consultant.

Ten Upright: A journey.
Reversed: Going across water.

Nine Upright: A will or a legacy.
Reversed: A troubled journey; delays.

Eight Upright: Affection of a 'club' man; good friend; ally.
Reversed: Papers; documents.

Seven Upright: Victory.
Reversed: Financial worry; delayed success or achievement.

Six Upright: Presents. Gifts.
Reversed: Ambition.

Five Upright: A lover.
Reversed: Flirtation.

Four Upright: Pleasure.
Reversed: Delays.

Three Upright: Economy (keep your money!).
Reversed: Position; honour.

Two Upright: Children.
Reversed: Letters.

Certain combinations may now be learned with these meanings or they may be left until later on, when the student has mastered simple card-reading. However, the brief meanings given above must be mastered, before any 'reading' is attempted.

Certain combinations

A Card 'with' one or two other cards, means that both or all three cards come out in the 'set-out' by either of the methods explained on pages 202–205.

The King of Hearts with the Nine of Hearts: A happy love.
The King of Hearts with the Ten of Hearts: Sincere love.
The Jack of Hearts with the Ten of Hearts: An ardent sweetheart.
The Jack of Hearts with the Nine of Hearts: An engagement.
The Eight of Hearts between Court Cards: Helpful friends.
Ten of Hearts with the Ace of Spades: A birth.
The Ace of Diamonds with the Eight of Hearts: An engagement ring.
The Two Black Tens: A long voyage.
King of Clubs with Ten of Hearts: True love of friends.
Jack of Diamonds with Ten of Spades: Trouble and unrest.
Ace of Diamonds with Ten of Hearts: A wedding.
Court Card with Seven of Spades: Treachery of a friend.
Diamond Court Card with Nine of Clubs: A rival in love.
Jack of Spades with Nine of Diamonds: A physician.
Jack of Spades with Nine of Clubs: A lawyer.
Ace of Spades with Nine of Hearts: Fulfilled longings (of the senses).
Ace of Spades with Nine of Clubs: A theatre. A place of public amusement.
The Ace of Spades touching a Queen with the Eight of Spades near: illicit meetings.

Duplicates of the same card

Kings

Four Kings	Upright: Honours; dignities. Reversed: Litigation.
Three Kings	Upright: Successful undertakings. Reversed: New projects.

Two Kings Upright: Friends in business.
Reversed: New projects.

Queens

Four Queens Upright: Quarrels; scandal.
Reversed: Frivolity.

Three Queens Upright: Society; convention.
Reversed: Scandal; gossip.

Two Queens Upright: Friendly consultations.
Reversed: Gossip.

Jacks

Four Jacks Upright: Treachery.
Reversed: A law court.

Three Jacks Upright: Disputes; affronts.
Reversed: Indifference.

Two Jacks Upright: A bill; a demand.
Reversed: False friends; treachery.

Tens

Four Tens Upright: Success.
Reversed: An unpleasant surprise.

Three Tens Upright: A happy future.
Reversed: Loss.

Two Tens Upright: A lucky surprise.
Reversed: Excesses.

Nines

Four Nines	Upright: Robbery; imposition. Reversed: Avarice; extreme greed.
Three Nines	Upright: Delay to projects. Reversed: Greed of gain.
Two Nines	Upright: (Red) – Riches: (Black) – Disappointment. Reversed: Loss.

Eights

Four Eights	Upright: Successful projects. Reversed: Disappointment; failure.
Three Eights	Upright: Thoughts of marriage. Reversed: Amusement; frivolity; flirtations.
Two Eights	Upright: Uncertain plans. Reversed: An undertaking, commitment.

Sevens

Four Sevens	Upright: Children. Reversed: Intrigues.
Three Sevens	Upright: Upset; disturbance. Reversed: Domestic worries.
Two Sevens	Upright: A proposal. Reversed: Worries.

Note that satisfactory card-reading can be accomplished by some methods without using the smaller cards. The Sixes, Fives, Fours, Threes, and Twos mostly stand for ideas. Their use belongs to more difficult divination by cards.

Sixes

Four Sixes Upright: Ambition.
Reversed: Wisdom.

Three Sixes Upright: Generosity.
Reversed: Wealth.

Two Sixes Upright: Gain.
Reversed: Joy.

Fives

Four Fives Upright: Caution.
Reversed: Caution against unfaithful allies.

Three Fives Upright: Power.
Reversed: Wealth.

Two Fives Upright: Anxiety.
Reversed: Speed.

Fours

Four Fours Upright: Pleasure.
Reversed: Cleverness.

Three Fours Upright: Catastrophe.
Reversed: Suspicion.

Two Fours Upright: Extravagance.
Reversed: Speculation.

Threes

Four Threes Upright: Strategy.
Reversed: Disappointment.

Three Threes Upright: Deception.
Reversed: Success

Two Threes Upright: Victory.
Reversed: Loss; obstacles; success delayed.

Twos

Four Twos Upright: News.
Reversed: Indifference.

Three Twos Upright: Alarm.
Reversed: Treachery.

Two Twos Upright: A small wish.
Reversed: Self-control.

The cut

You may cut the cards on every occasion, before beginning to comb out the cards that are to form the 'fortune' proper, by dealing them according to either of the following methods:

To cut – shuffle the cards well and put them into three lots, face upwards. Red cards are 'bright' cards, and are better than black cards. Two reds out of three cards are better than the other way about, that is, two black and one red.

But remember that Clubs are never bad. Although the Spades are not bad either, generally, they are not a cheerful suit.

Read the meanings of the Cards you have cut, reminding the

subject (or yourself if you are telling your own fortune) that what is told by the cut may be in the distant future, and that it may be avoided if it is not good. The cut is true, yet it is not sure to come true! It has significance as a warning or a promise. But if the same cards reappear in the 'set-out' or 'fortune,' then their early fulfilment is emphasised.

Two simple methods of card-reading

You may now begin to cut the cards for yourself, that is, to tell your own fortune; for this will give you proficiency in handling, in reading, and in 'telling'. The first method makes use of all the cards in the pack.

Choose as 'yourself' a Queen if you are a woman, a King if a married man, a Jack if a single man. Choose the suit according to your complexion.

Shuffle the 52 cards well, and, if you are using a new pack, turn some of them about a few times, to get the 'reverse' meanings, if these want to come out.

Then deal the cards out one by one, saying as you turn each one up on the heap before you: 'King, Queen, Jack, Ten, Nine, Eight, Seven, Six, Five, Four, Three, Two, One, Heart'. (We give the Hearts an extra chance in each of the thirteen chances, because Hearts are always good, and human nature craves good news).

If a King of any suit comes out as you say 'King', put it out above the heap and begin again – 'King, Queen,' etc. If a Queen comes out when you say 'Queen,' a Two when you say 'two,' an Ace when you say 'one' or a Heart, when you say 'Heart', always put the agreeing card out, and always begin again, saying the list in order of value. You would have to begin again when you say 'Heart' whether an agreeing card came out or not, for Heart is the last of the line.

When you have gone through the pack, take up the cards that have been thrown out again. However, do not begin with 'King' unless the last card was in agreement with your call and was put above in the 'fortune'. If your last card thrown in the heap was a Six, begin with 'five' when you commence to deal for the second time.

Repeat the deal a third time. That is, comb out the 'fortune' proper by three dealings of the cards that have not agreed with your calling of the List, the discarded cards.

The disadvantage of this first method is that you may get very few cards out. In that case, things are probably going very uneventfully with you. Tell yourself 'Happy is the nation that has no History!'

Great or important events are not imminent, either, if you have quite a lot of cards of the smaller values, that is the 'under sevens'. Dealings with people are rare, if Picture Cards are absent or are few in the 'set-out'.

A lot of Picture Cards means company, or that you are going to meet people, even if festivity is not implied. But you may expect small worries if the small cards are mostly dark ones, especially if Spades predominate.

Spades are (roughly) anxieties, if not actual troubles.
Hearts are love, company, visiting, the home and pleasure.
Diamonds represent money and business matters.
Clubs, though black, are good and stand for success, power and achievement.

Spades and Diamonds are 'chancy' suits. You cannot help or

alter or avoid the things for which they stand; and a lot of Diamonds, although they represent money, do not exactly mean money earned or money which you can increase.Hearts and Clubs are happier, more pleasant suits.

If, however, 'you' (the card that stands for 'yourself') come out, you can control the indications in the 'set-out'; you can improve matters if there are a lot of Spades in your 'fortunes'; and you can increase the good promise of the Hearts or Clubs that have come out.

The Nine of Hearts is the best card in the pack; the Nine of Spades the worst. When this last is 'out' by this first method and 'you' are not out, you must just 'sit tight'; do not attempt to do things – if you do, your efforts will come to nothing.

Remind yourself that the Cards may tell a brighter tale in a day or two.

Now read the Cards you have combed out – they may be three or they may be thirty-three – by this dealing of the whole pack three times. Keep in mind the simple meanings you have learned.

The Second Method

In this second method you only use the cards above the Sixes, that is the four Aces, Kings, Queens, Jacks, Tens, Nines, Eights, and Sevens.

Shuffle the 32 cards and deal, counting each card you throw out thus, 'One, two, three, four, five, six'. Put the seventh card in a line above the heap of discarded cards. Count six again and throw them out, add the seventh card to the first above. Repeat until you have only four cards in your hand.

Count these and throw them out, pick up the discards again and go on, saying 'five, six, seven'; place this third one out above; count six and put the seven always in the line above the discarded cards. On this occasion your last card will be the seventh and should be placed in the line above. Then pick up the pile of discards and continue counting and placing the seventh card in the line above until you are left with three cards. Count these out and pick up the discards counting out 'four, five, six'; the seventh card will be placed above and the rest of the pack set aside leaving you with twelve cards for the fortune reading.

Notice whether it is the black or red cards that predominate. Read the combinations and then 'read the fortune'.

Do not read these twelve cards one by one, as in the first method. Count to the seventh and then count to the fourteenth, which will be the third from the first card at the left hand. Count on from seven from this, and add its meaning to the seven further on, going back always to the beginning, or the first card at your left. Do this, getting six (double-card) meanings, as you end on the twelfth or last card in the 'set-out'.

If you want to get more from the reading, you may now couple the cards, reading the first and the twelfth, the second and the eleventh, the third and the tenth, and so on until the last pair, the sixth and the seventh, have been read in conjunction.

When you become more skilful, you may shuffle the twenty smaller cards and add one of them to each of your 'couples'. But remember that these twelve cards are the 'Fortune' proper, and that the small cards are only used to obtain further light on what the six 'pairs' tell you.

Note that this second method gives you more of a story to tell, owing to the linking up of the meanings of two cards every time.

You can get to be a reliable card-reader, with constant practice of these two easy methods.

Advanced card reading

You may stick to these two methods and extract all that is to be got out of the cards, although there are very many more systems. Some of these are very intricate indeed.

The secret of success, provided you are intelligent, sincere and sympathetic, is to know the meanings of the cards in the very fullest sense.

Here are the more involved shades of meanings. However, first note that each of the 52 cards can be allotted to each of the 52 weeks in the year.

You can get your 'Luck of the Week', by one single cut of your cards. It is not necessarily 'Bad Luck' if you do not cut 'the Card of the Week'. It means a deservedly successful week if you cut 'yourself', especially if you have Clubs with you, for then the success is earned.

But a really bright and shining success is indicated if you cut 'the Card of the Week', as listed below.

It will prove advantageous to learn these meanings, and all the deeper possibilities, as given in this advanced style of card-reading. You will find yourself gaining a tremendous amount of knowledge, if you use the methods you have already learned after you have memorised the meanings of the cards of each week in the year.

Note that the weeks of the year are not read always from Sunday to Saturday in this connection; but always according to what day New Year's Day falls on. Thus 'the Week' may be from Tuesday to Monday if New Year's Day was on Tuesday; from Friday to Thursday, if 1 January was a Friday and so on.

The cards of the weeks

'I,' is for the first week in January and is represented by the Seven of Hearts. The rest follow in sequence as in this list:

I	The Seven of Hearts
II	The King of Clubs
III	The Eight of Diamonds
IV	The Ace of Hearts
V	The Five of Clubs
VI	The Three of Spades
VII	The Nine of Hearts
VIII	The Two of Clubs
IX	The Queen of Diamonds
X	The Jack of Spades
XI	The Ten of Clubs
XII	The Four of Diamonds
XIII	The Two Of Spades
XIV	The Nine of Diamonds
XV	The King of Hearts
XVI	The Eight of Spades
XVII	The Six of Clubs
XVIII	The Seven of Diamonds
XIX	The Three of Hearts
XX	The Ten of Spades
XXI	The Jack of Clubs
XXII	The Ten of Hearts
XXIII	The Six of Diamonds
XXIV	The Queen of Spades
XXV	The Four of Hearts
XXVI	The Ace of Clubs

XXVII	The King of Diamonds
XXVIII	The Five of Spades
XXIX	The Three of Diamonds
XXX	The Jack of Hearts
XXXI	The Queen of Hearts
XXXII	The Four of Clubs
XXXIII	The Ace of Spades
XXXIV	The Nine of Clubs
XXXV	The Five of Hearts
XXXVI	The Eight of Clubs
XXXVII	The Ten of Diamonds
XXXVIII	The Two of Hearts
XXXIX	The Six of Spades
XL	The Seven of Clubs
XLI	The Jack of Diamonds
XLII	The Four of Spades
XLIII	The Six of Hearts
XLIV	The Queen of Clubs
XLV	The Two of Diamonds
XLVI	The Nine of Spades
XLVII	The Ace of Diamonds
XLVIII	The Seven of Spades
XLIX	The Five of Diamonds
L	The Three of Clubs
LI	The King of Spades
LII	The Eight of Hearts

Note that the Nine of Hearts should come as near as possible to St Valentine's Day (14 February) and that the Nine of Spades properly belongs to the dreary month of November.

Another simple method

The subject should shuffle the thirty-two cards, leaving out the Sixes, Fives, Fours, Threes, and Twos, and cut them into three groups. Let the seer take up the first pack and ask the subject to pick out three cards. These are to stand for the past. The second group is then to be taken up and the subject will pick out five cards, to represent the present. From the third group seven cards are to be picked to represent the future. These are to be read in the light of the meanings given.

Further light may be thrown on the cards selected if each of the three, five, and seven cards respectively, are covered by one of the cards of smaller value. However, it is to be remembered that the 'fortune' proper is read in the cards selected, which include only those from the Sevens to the Aces.

To wish (by cards)

Shall I get my wish?

Define the wish in your own mind; shuffle the cards, keeping the Wish clearly before you.

Cut once, and note the card you cut.

Deal the whole pack into three lots or heaps.

Now take up each group and look for the card you cut. If it comes in the same lot as 'yourself', the answer is 'yes'.

If it comes with 'yourself' and if the Wish Card, the Nine of Hearts, is in the same lot, then it is 'yes', with great success or joy. If the Wish Card comes between 'yourself' and the card you cut, you will get your wish with Love.

If the Wish Card appears in the lot with 'yourself', but the card you cut is not in that group, this means you will not obtain what you actually wished for, but probably something that is better for you.

If the Nine of Spades comes in the same group with the card you cut, and 'yourself' also, a great disappointment is in store for you, although you do obtain this wish.

If the Nine of Spades comes with the card you cut, and 'you' do not come in that group, you will not obtain what you want, but rather will feel bitter disappointment.

You do not get your wish unless 'you' and the card you cut while wishing are in the same group; and if there are many cards between these two cards, so much time will elapse before the wish comes true.

The nearer these two cards are to each other, when they are in the one lot, the sooner will the wish come true.

Note that something good involving a surprise is promised if the card you cut in order to know if you will get your wish by this method, happens to be the 'Card of the Week'.

Involved meanings

Now learn the more involved meanings of each card. Note that, while some of these differ from the simple meanings you have learned already, they do not contradict them. When you can link both of them, you will be a really proficient card-reader.

Two of Spades

This card signifies a removal. If 'you' do not appear in the same 'set-out', you will hear of a friend whose removal will bring him or her nearer to you. It does not stand for a rich or very powerful friend. If reversed, it means that one you now call a friend will, before long, become your enemy.

But this meaning of an enemy in the guise of a friend more properly belongs to the meanings of small cards – those below the Sevens – when used to confirm or modify the meanings of the weightier cards – Sevens and upwards – around them. Thus, this Two of Spades coming up against the King of Hearts, a fairish or light-brown-haired-man – whom you can identify – shows he is your friend, though you may have been doubting him lately. The Two, if reversed, indicates that this particular friend is failing you in some way.

To hold two Twos gives you a small wish. Take advantage of it at once, noting whether the next card you turn up is black or red. If red, the answer is 'yes'. But if the black card is a Club it is not an unfavourable answer, though it stands for 'no'.

Note that cards of small value must always be interpretation in relation to the meanings of the weightier cards near them, and that if cut they stand for comparatively insignificant happenings.

Three of Spades

This card tells of a quarrel; but if 'you' are out with it, it is a quarrel in which you have the advantage. You are going to turn what looks like failure into success at the last minute. People who do this are never 'down' for long, especially if they resolve to hold all they gain.

This Three of Spades near the Ace of Hearts speaks of quarrels at home; if near the Ace of Spades it tells of business disputes. Near a Picture Card, it signifies anger with someone of that significance. But these are not important or angry quarrels, just disputes, contradictions, and foolish wrangling – irritation rather than passionate anger.

If reversed, this card tells of confusion, doubt, and apprehension. Delay any important enterprise if this card is in your hand, for the affair will be hindered by distrust and insecurity.

Four of Spades

If you cut this card, be prepared for sickness or for trouble in some form. This is not a good card. Even with good cards on both sides of it when it comes out in the 'set-out', it foretells loneliness and sadness of the heart. (An infallible cure for this evil is to go out and do someone a good turn!)

If reversed, This Four of Spades speaks definitely of a sick-bed. But if next to a Court Card of some other signification than 'yourself', the sickness will be for a person of that sex and colouring - yet it may be disastrous for you, in some way, that this person should be ill at this particular time.

Five of Spades

If you cut this Five of Spades, you are thereby warned to correct your bad temper! This is emphasised still more if it comes out in your 'fortune'.

You are jeopardising your own interest by indulging either your anger, jealousy or spite, or even hatred, unjustifiably.

Heed the warning and question yourself honestly: you may find that your anger is undeserved or your jealousy unwarranted.

If this Five of Spades comes out reversed, you will certainly be surprised, and not pleasantly so. This surprise also refers to the matter in which your anger has been misleading you.

It may be that this ugly little card promises you mourning. This is one of the least happy of its meanings. Be warned in time, or you will mourn indeed.

Six of Spades

This card says you will take a voyage or a journey towards water sooner than you expect. It will not be a prosperous journey nor one which you can make profitable. For Spades, even when they are not bad, stand for fatalistic things.

When it comes out near to Picture Cards, the Six of Spades tells of a voyage or of travelling towards the sea relating to some person or persons of the colour and sex indicated by the Court Card.

If reversed, this card warns you of a surprise in connection with a voyage or a place near water. It will not be a very unpleasant surprise, unless other Spades are on either side of this Six.

Seven of Spades

This card tells of a removal or change or upset, which you should avoid if possible. Spades are not a good suit, and Sevens stand for displacement or some kind of change. If you cut this Seven reversed, be very watchful over your tongue and your temper, and look closely into the actions of all third parties concerning themselves with you and with one you love. For this card threatens the loss of one dear to you, with much trouble, if reversed – not a loss through death, but by estrangement or interference or because of the hate, malice, or jealousy of others.

This is never of good omen. If near to the Nine of Diamonds, you will hear of an accident; with the Nine of Spades also near, the person who has been injured may die.

Eight of Spades

This card stands for the night and illness, but if it comes out with good cards around it, some extraordinary things may happen in the night; yet your safety will not be seriously threatened. Between a King and Queen, this card foretells of a matrimonial separation; near but not separating them, a danger of trouble of this kind. Between two Kings, this Eight warns of the alienation of business friends. With the Nine of Diamonds, business trouble is still more clearly indicated.

If you have two Eights in your fortune, or if you cut two Eights in succession, you are advised to drop all idea of an illusion, or dream, or project, or ambition which attracts you at the present time. If you do not drop it, it will drop you, or fail you painfully. This warning applies especially to a 'Love Dream' – that is, the hope of attracting to yourself the love of a certain person who has no thought of you in connection with love. Women, in particular, should accept this warning of the two Eights if they wish to avoid rebuffs or slights which would hurt their feelings. However, a man should also heed the warning. If he is indulging in hopes which will not come to fruition, this warning may be valuable to him. The appearance of two Eights between Diamonds signify a false dream of money gains.

Spades, generally, have a sad significance, although with good cards near, they may speak only of delays to the happy events promised by the other cards.

Nine of Spades

If you cut this card at any time, your Luck is out. Do not try any new venture or tread any new ground until a week has passed. If you do, failure and disappointment will dog your footsteps.

If it lies between Heart cards, this ill-omened Nine of Spades tells of failure sweetened by Love. But if other Spades flank the Heart cards, it is illicit love and the end is evil! Between Diamonds, this Nine tells of poverty to be followed by riches. Between Clubs, of disappointment to be followed by success.

Next to, or near to, the Nine of Diamonds you will hear bad

news of a death; next or near to the Seven of Diamonds then an accident, which may result in the death of the injured person.

Ten of Spades

This warns you of imminent unhappiness, grief, or sickness – perhaps of a mixture of all three evils!

If it comes in a 'set-out' with the Five of Spades before or after it, you are about to suffer a bereavement. With the Jack of Spades next to or near it when you have set out your cards, trouble or unrest is indicated. However, if it is held side by side with the other black Ten, a voyage – not necessarily an unhappy voyage – is surely going to be taken. Note that the two black Tens betoken a really long journey overseas, and not a mere cruise.

With the Nine of Diamonds, illness, probably accompanied by an operation is indicated. With the Nine of Spades flanking these, the sick person may be in considerable danger.

Jack of Spades

This is not a good card to cut, unless you are a very dark unmarried man, when, it stands for 'yourself', and tells you to press forward with your plans – you are sure to win.

With another Knave he tells of deceit. Even if they are the two red Knaves, two Knaves represent deceit. Three Knaves together forecast dishonesty, swindling, often 'Big Business' frauds. Be warned – if you are connected with people whom you suspect of being far 'too clever' in business, cut your ties with them before they tarnish your good name or your credit. If your own affairs are safe, you will hear of unscrupulous dealings in financial circles when these three Knaves turn up together.

The Jack of Spades with the Queen of Spades, when both reversed, speaks of scandal. You will hear tell of domestic trouble among your married friends if you deal such a combination in your fortune.

If you cannot place a personal explanation on the Knave of Spades, he may stand for 'the night'. Thus, the King of Hearts and the Ten of Spades (sickness) warn you of a dear friend taken ill during the night, when this Knave is near them.

Queen of Spades

This card is generally taken to mean a very dark woman. However, if you the card reversed, it is taken to represent a malicious woman, one whom it is certainly not safe to trust. Alternatively it can signify a melancholy or bad-tempered person, either dark or fair. Be warned against such a woman, whatever her complexion, and say as little as possible when you are next in her company.

With her Jack, this Queen of Spades promises scandal as well as plots. Either a married woman of your acquaintance is playing with fire, or a married man is pursuing some woman other than his wife. In either case this combination indicates that the parties are running a considerable risk of being discovered.

There is a significant danger of scandal to 'you' if these two cards of evil omen – the Queen and Jack of Spades – are next or near to the Picture Card which signifies 'yourself'.

King of Spades

This card says you will hear of, or from, a public or 'Government man'; a man of affairs such as a banker, lawyer, stockbroker, head of a public department, or of a big firm; or perhaps he is a Member of Parliament?

If reversed, he is either troubled, worried, angry, or not so friendly to you as he was or as you believe him to be. Look to the cards next or near to him, in order to know more about this important man and his connection with your affairs. If reversed, and between Diamonds, he is bothered about money; between Hearts, about his domestic affairs – or yours, if the card signifying 'you' intervenes. The conjunction of Hearts with Spades stands for sensual pleasures. With Clubs, this card reversed, says that his ambition is slow in being rewarded; with other Spades disappointment or failure, or it may even be that death threatens him. This is certainly the case if the Nine of Spades touches him.

Ace of Spades

This card promises Big Business, especially if it subsequently appears with Diamonds near. If reversed, the Ace of Spades warns you that news of a death is coming to you. If it is next to the Nine of Diamonds, it tells of a death caused by an accident.

The Ace of Spades with Hearts near implies sensual pleasures.

If this Ace comes between Hearts, you will be involved in a violent love affair. Next or near to the Nine of Clubs, you will go to a theatre. This Ace of Spades between a King and Queen signifies an illicit union or unlawful connection.

The Ace of Spades means a high building, probably an office block, when you are reading a fortune that is mainly concerned with business matters. This is especially so when the Ace of Hearts is out also. The two Aces will give you 'The Home' and 'The Office', but remember that two Aces always mean new plans.

Two of Diamonds

This is one of the small cards which means a big thing. If you cut it, you will receive a considerable sum of money, and if it comes in your 'set-out', the money is as good as in your hands.

However, if reversed, with a Court Card near, its significance is: 'Do not keep your present engagement, whether it concerns money or love' – that is, the last engagement you made or the one you should otherwise keep within 24 hours of cutting this card. You will certainly be surprised or startled in the matter of this particular engagement, whether you keep it or not!

Three of Diamonds

This card says: 'Watch your domestic affairs'. If it comes out next to 'yourself', act with caution and prudence, for scandal is buzzing about you. This card says 'be discreet', or else it suggests that you should warn your partner to be more guarded as to his or her conduct.

If the unmarried cut this Three of Diamonds, it denotes that they will shortly be speaking with a friend, and quarrels concerning business or money or legal matters are likely to follow.

Four of Diamonds

This card indicates some kind of trouble through friends. The Four of Diamonds always stands for company, mixing with more people than usual, making new acquaintances. But this company is, as a rule, business or 'duty' company; it does not include socialising or celebration, though many Hearts around this card would modify this last meaning. In this case, business gathering with celebration is indicated. This does happen occasionally.

This Four of Diamonds has some kind of a warning of a secret betrayed. Hear everything and say nothing when you are in company after having cut this card.

Next to a Club, this card stands for a car – still with a warning!

Two Fours together convey a hint that you should check extravagance. When reversed they point to speculation. They do not say 'Cease to speculate', but only 'Be careful'.

Three Fours together are not a good omen. It indicates catastrophe of some sort. If you draw them, remember catastrophic events may still turn out well, in the long run. Diamonds stand for things you cannot alter or help. Sit tight, keep your head cool, and cultivate the long view, if your fortune shows three Fours or even if you should cut them one after the other. In this latter case, only a warning as to probable catastrophe is the meaning.

Five of Diamonds

This card tells of a settlement with regard to some money matter with which you are concerned – not necessarily a large sum of money unless with other and larger Diamond cards, or with that important little money card, the Two of Diamonds, around. The settlement will be unexpected or you will have a surprise in connection with it.

In a set-out in which 'you' do not appear, the meaning is the same; but the settlement is not so directly for 'you', unless the card signifying yourself has been first cut. If reversed, this card signifies the law or legal proceedings and the successful ending is delayed.

Six of Diamonds

This card, when cut, speaks of hope and promises pleasure. But if it should be reversed, it threatens trouble from people beneath you, if you are in business.

If it comes up reversed in your 'fortune' and next to a King or a Queen, it says that the person denoted by the Picture Card will be widowed early in life.

The single man or woman who cuts it reversed, and finds it next or near to a Picture Card, will surely hear of the death of a dear friend's wife or husband; this will be an untimely death.

Seven of Diamonds

If you cut this card, you are thereby warned that friends – or some of those whom you look upon as friends – are speaking evil of you.

If the Jack of Hearts comes next or near to this card, you are going to hear of a birth. If the Jack and the Queen of Spades are in the same fortune by cards as this Seven, grave scandal is threatened.

The seven of Diamonds is not a good card.

Eight of Diamonds

The Eight of Diamonds stands for remarriage. If you cut it, you are either going to receive attentions from a widower, or to propose to a widow; or you are certain to hear of somebody making a second venture into matrimony.

Diamonds signify money. They also represent casual, haphazard, 'chancy' things. If you have made a deal involving money, this card promises success – but it is not a success 'you' can engineer or influence by any effort on your behalf. It speaks of hope but of blind hope. It gives no place to will or work.

If a Spade is next to this card, beware of danger or accident. However, if it is a Club, money and business are better. If it is a Heart, friendship helps greatly, especially if it is a Heart card of high significance.

Nine of Diamonds

This card foretells of unexpectedly good business, though it is business your skill cannot influence.

Yet the actual meaning of the Nine of Diamonds is anger, wounds, weapons; you must always read it in this connection if it appears in your fortune by cards. If next to, or near the Nine of Spades, you will hear of the death of a friend who has undergone an operation recently, or who has sustained an injury an accident.

Next to a Queen, this card tells of a woman who will undergo an operation; with Hearts near, it indicates that this will be successful. If near the Ten of Hearts, it tells of the safe birth of a child to a woman of the colouring of the Queen, who has, nevertheless, been in some danger. If the Nine of Diamonds is cut near two black Tens, the card tells of news of an operation on someone a great distance away. When the King of Diamonds comes up with it, he always represents a doctor; similarly, the King of Spades is a lawyer or banker, in this connection.

With Clubs near it, this Nine tells of anger over business matters, but they are not, otherwise, unfortunate business matters. With the Ace of Spades, a serious quarrel over business.

Ten of Diamonds

It is a very auspicious sign to cut this card. The Ten of Diamonds stands for money; a good round sum of money, although not the largest sum you can receive, in connection with any deal or business venture in which you are interested. The little Two of Diamonds means a larger sum still.

Two Red Tens together signify a lucky surprise in connection with money. But if both are reversed, you will be in touch with prosperous and charming people who are over-inclined to look on the wine when it is red.

Resolve not to share in their excesses.

Jack of Diamonds

This card says you may look for important written communications.

For a very fair or red-headed bachelor to cut it, his luck is in – he may do big things, and these will undoubtedly turn out well, for this Knave stands for 'himself'.

If next to another Picture Card, the sex and colouring of the sender of the weighty messages may be deduced.

The matter of the letter or communication may be read from adjacent cards. Hearts signify things social and of romantic attachment; Spades, sickness or anxiety; Diamonds, money; Clubs, stand for things that have been long desired and fought for.

Queen of Diamonds

This card signifies either a very fair or a red- or white-haired woman. If you are a fair girl, it is 'you', and it is always exceptionally lucky either to cut 'yourself' or to have the card of your own signification come out. It means that you can control any matter in which you are interested; that you may act this week, without fear. If you are married, the King of Diamonds is your husband, whatever colour your husband may actually be. If you are not a fair woman, this represents a good woman of that complexion unless she comes up with Spades. If she is reversed, she is a flirt and is unreliable.

With the King of Diamonds, this tells of a married couple; but if the Nine of Hearts is with them, you will hear of the engagement of this fair woman very shortly. Any Diamond Court Card with the Nine of Clubs, says you have a rival in love.

King of Diamonds

If you cut this card, you will certainly have reason to see a doctor or you will have some business with a medical man. The business does not necessarily signify anxiety – to cut a Picture Card always indicates friends; Kings are generally powerful friends.

This King of Diamonds stands for a very fair man, a red-haired man or a grey-headed one.

If reversed, he may be an enemy or a treacherous person. More frequently, an enemy in business. You see how true it is that Diamonds are 'chancy' things. When they mean good fortunes, there is an element of uncertainty about it. Yet Diamonds stand for the morning and for youth and hope too. But these are uncertain and impermanent.

Ace of Diamonds

When this card is cut, it indicates that you can expect to receive money through the post; cheques, notes, etc. When reversed, it tells that a letter about money, perhaps containing news of money, is being delayed although it is coming to you. Next to a Court Card, the money comes from a person of the sex and colouring of the Court Card's meaning.

If the Ace of Diamonds is with the King and the Nine of Hearts, it promises you the offer of a ring and says that you will make a prosperous marriage; of course that is if 'you' are also held in the hand. If 'you' are absent, the monied marriage is for the person indicated by the surrounding cards. Or it will be within your reach but you look on the opportunity with indifference.

Two of Hearts

A visit from a lover. If reversed, the opposition to a love affair; or, if with Clubs, the opposition of those who love you to some project with which you want to push on.

A man or woman in business may expect someone who loves him or her to come to the home, office or place of work.

Three of Hearts

This card promises success, but if reversed you may be careful that your own imprudence in the past, in connection with seeking this change, does not cause you sorrow.

With another Heart near it in your 'set-out' of cards, the Three of Hearts tells of achievement. Next to a Picture Card, of a kiss from a person of the sex and complexion shown by the Court Card.

Two Threes side by side tell of victory in connection with some comparatively small matter about which you have been anxious. Two Red Threes, of joy with the victory. But if one of the two Threes is a black Spade, there will be jealousy, which will take some of the pleasure from your triumph.

Four of Hearts

Although this card means a messenger, it stands for stubbornness in connection with a matter on which you will receive a message.

If next or near to 'yourself' (the Picture Card signifying 'you') you are being stubborn about some matter on which you are pushing to get your own way because it is your own way and not because it is the right way. Ask yourself if it would not be better to put your obstinacy aside and begin again?

If next or near to the card which signifies the person on whom you have fixed your affection, this person will be hard to win indeed! But Hearts cannot carry a really bad meaning. This comparatively insignificant Four of Hearts may serve to convey a message, having some reference to stubbornness – a stubborn aim or a stubborn person rather than a really persevering one.

Five of Hearts

This card has to do with married love, but it promises that the subject will suffer through jealousy. If cut in the week to which it belongs, this Five of Hearts tells you that you are sure to receive a present before long. But if it comes out next to a Ten of any suit, an invitation is promised.

Near a King and Queen, you are going to be surprised by news of a marriage. If near Diamonds, a good change in money matters is promised. If the Five of Hearts is near any Clubs, you will reap the result of your efforts and of your perseverance in the past – the amount will be according to the number or dignity of the cards. As a general rule, though, cards of small value rarely promise big events or successes.

Six of Hearts

Speaks of the reappearance in your life of an old lover or of someone who, long ago, paid you attention – this person will proceed to court you in earnest now. When reversed, this Six of Hearts tells of some attempt to trick you. It is not a villain who will try to do this, but a rather good-hearted though distinctly 'tricky' person. We all know this type – people who would rather run crookedly than straight, even when to go straight would be less trouble! Look out for such a person and ignore any attempt they might make to rush you into a particular line of action.

Let 'masterly inactivity' be your motto. If properly carried out, you cannot be beaten while you practise this policy.

Seven of Hearts

This card tells us of something that is not lasting – a gain in money matters which will be fairly short-lived, or an increase in one's income which will not be as good as it first sounds. It may be a small success in connection with social affairs – something temporary. Look at the cards on each side to find out more about the matter.

If reversed, the Seven of Hearts tells of the jealousy of women. Again, the matter on which this jealousy turns must be interpreted from the cards that surround it. However, although they may refer to passion, Hearts are never entirely bad.

Eight of Hearts

This card, which belongs to the last week in the dying year, tells of a mind at ease and of a good, friendly feeling surrounding you. The key-significance of this Eight of Hearts is thoughts – happy thinking, generous thinking; and this is indeed a good sign to close the passing year and with which to open the unknown days of the New Year.

This Eight has a further message of happy spending, perhaps of buying new clothes which will please you. Next or near to the Ace of Diamonds, the meaning is an engagement ring in the coming year, with happy spending of money in furniture, dress, etc., in the immediate time following on the engagement. Further, it implies company, feasting, and so on.

Note that, while Eight is the number of movement and change, the good omen of the Hearts is stronger that the uncertainty indicated by the number. Happy changes, due to love, are promised by this Eight of Hearts, whatever week in the year it is cut or dealt out in the 'set-out'.

Nine of Hearts

This is the best card in the pack. It stands, first and foremost, for love; happy love, success in love or triumphant love. Therefore, it is fittingly associated with the Feast of St Valentine, the patron of true lovers. This fateful date is was celebrated long before it became the name-day of the gentle Christian saint. St Valentine's Day is actually the old Roman feast of the Lupercalia, of the goddess of fertility, of the blooming of life.

This Nine of Hearts also stands for success. If you cut it in the first half of February, or if it is dealt to you, be sure to 'wish on it' as you touch it. You will succeed in love, if love is what you are keen on at the moment. Success with money is indicated if Diamonds are on either side, when you tell your fortune. Success in your ambitions is indicated if Clubs are near this lucky card. With the Knave of Hearts it denotes an engagement. With a King and Queen of the same suit, a wedding. These combinations with the Ace of Hearts tell of an engagement or a wedding at your home. With the card that signifies 'you', the engagement or the wedding is for you. This card near the Ace of Hearts promises a celebration at your house.

Ten of Hearts

The Ten of Hearts promises domestic and family happiness – a good change if there has been recent anxiety in connection with social or financial matters. The Ten of Hearts neutralises the effects of evil cards near it, and it strengthens and confirms good omens. This is its general meaning.

The Ten of Hearts has a more particular significance associated with pleasure, a place of amusement or a party. If a Ten of Hearts comes next to the Ace of Spades, you are going to a theatre; next to a King, to a dinner party; next to a Queen, a formal evening function, if you are a man. The Ten of Hearts next to a Queen, in a fortune by cards told for a woman, tells her that she can expect to receive something very pleasant through the post. Between a Queen and a King, the card signifies a happy event, an addition to the family, is foretold. Next to a Queen, a very ardent lover; for a single man, a sweetheart who is young.

The Ten of Hearts promises change, but it is invariably a very good change which is indicated.

Jack of Hearts

This card speaks of love and the thoughts of the loved one which are active about you.

The Knave of Hearts stands for one who is beloved, of either sex. It promises a young man or woman a speedy and happy engagement. If it is next or near to the Nine of Diamonds, it tells of a quarrel with the beloved; if next or near to the Nine of Spades, it speaks of misfortune to the loved one.

If those who are not concerned with love and lovemaking cut this card, or it comes out in their 'fortune', it promises them much joy through the natural affections of the heart, which belong to every age and time of life.

Queen of Hearts

It is very lucky indeed for a woman with warm golden or chestnut hair to cut this card, for it stands for 'herself' and promises her that she may safely embark on any enterprise with sure hopes of success. She may also accept any opportunity that presents itself.

When this card comes out as part of the fortune, it means that the subject will hear news of a woman of the colouring represented. If it appears next to the Jack of Hearts, there will be news of an engagement; on one side of the Nine of Hearts, with the King on the other side, a happy marriage. The King and Queen of any suit mean, for a business man, a partnership or agreement. The Queen of Hearts next to the Ace of Spades stands for an actress. If it is reversed, there will be news of a handsome but changeable woman, rather than an affectionate woman, which the card represents when it comes out the right way up.

King of Hearts

This is an extraordinarily good card for anyone. If it should be cut for a married man of this colouring – fairish or light brown – there is scarcely anything he may not dare to do.

The King of Hearts with the Nine of Hearts tells of an engagement; with the Ten of Hearts, indicating a happy marriage.

Two Kings together in your fortune by cards signify an important business meeting which is being held about this time and which will ultimately increase your financial prosperity. Two Kings reversed say that new business ventures must be closely watched if they are to prove successful. (Remember, you can only read King as 'reversed' if you have put 'R' for reversed in the top, left-hand corner.) If you do not specifically identify the King of Hearts as a relative, friend or lover, its general meaning is of a good, loving man, with a rather hasty temper. If reversed, this indicates that he is inclined to be fickle.

Note that the King of Hearts must always stand for the husband of a married woman who is 'between colours', when her cards are being read, whatever colour her husband may be.

Ace of Hearts

The card stands for the house. If reversed, it stands for a change of residence, a holiday or merely 'a strange bed' for a night or two for the person whose cards are being read.

A keen businessman or woman may take the Ace of Hearts to mean the office.

A Picture Card near and facing towards the Ace, means that a person of the sex and colouring indicated by the picture is coming to your house; facing away from the Ace, such a person is going away from the place. With the Ace of Spades near, the visit concerns business. The Ten of Hearts near this Ace indicates a party or a celebration in your home. When the Knave and Nine of Hearts are near, this indicates an engagement for someone in the home; the King with the Ten promises a wedding. A red King with his Queen also indicates a wedding; a black King and Queen show a partnership. If these are Spades, the business of the partnership will involve some anxiety.

The Queen and Knave of Spades near the Ace of Hearts tell of scandalous conduct. Two Kings in the same fortune as this card show an important business conference. Depending on how near they are near to the Ace, this will mean more success for the subjects domestic or professional interests.

Two of Clubs

This card stands for letters. The cards of small value – Sixes and under – are not important, but the smallest cards have their meanings, and these should be read in conjunction with the cards that lie alongside of them. This card says you are going to handle important letters. With two Kings the letters will be about a business meeting; with two Queens, about committee meetings or other mundane gatherings. With the Ace of Spades and the Nine of Clubs, letters about a theatre or a theatrical venture. But the letters decide nothing. This small card promises nothing definite.

Two Twos together in a hand of cards warn you to exercise self-control in a matter that will soon be in progress. Three Twos convey a hint of treachery; while four Twos tell you to expect very striking developments concerning a matter, though small and unimportant enough in itself.

Three of Clubs

If you cut this card, your position, with regard to some matter which had threatened it, has been stabilised. But you will do well to practise economy, for you are not yet out of the woods nor quite secure in your holding or position or job. If this card comes out in a 'set-out' among pictures, you will hear of one of your friends making a second marriage late in life; a very prudent, worldly-wise 'look-to-the-future' sort of arrangement it will be. To identify the blushing elderly bride or bridegroom, look to the Picture Card next or near to this Three.

Among reversed cards, this Three of Clubs stands for quarrelling about a post or worldly affairs – small and rather insignificant affairs, for the Three is a small number. But Clubs always stand for effort, success, 'getting there', and when they are reversed only delay is indicated.

Four of Clubs

This card promises pleasures, but only on a small or insignificant scale, and with some relation to business. If reversed, the Four of Clubs speaks of delays to a pleasure already arranged, or perhaps of some little hitch in the arrangements. Next to a Picture Card in a 'set-out', this card promises a journey or a business deal, involving a car or cars, with a person of the sex and colouring indicated by the Picture Card.

To anyone involved in important business, this card says: 'Be prudent and you will succeed; but the success you gain will bring you satisfaction rather than a real increase in money.'

Five of Clubs

This card suggests a new lover. If the cards around it are of small value, an engagement or marriage with the stranger is not promised. If Spades are near, guard yourself against treachery or deception from someone professing a regard for you.

A girl cutting it reversed may indeed walk warily. A man who cuts this card will find that a lady whom he looks upon as a friend has a wish to be something more – she wants to tempt him from his present commitment.

If reversed and set between a King and Queen of the same suit, this card tells you of matrimonial reactions disturbing married friends. But with good cards around, the rift will not widen; they will 'kiss again with tears'.

Six of Clubs

This card promises gifts. It bodes well for your ambition, too, but with bad cards near, it warns you against someone who is soon to give you a valuable present.

If near the Ace of Diamonds in a young person's hand, it tells of the gift of a ring; for older people a valuable present of something round – a bracelet, a belt, or an oval cigarette-case or tie-band. Yet one should always read of this present in connection with ambition or business.

Two Sixes tell of gain, and even though they might be reversed, they promise a joy of some kind.

Three Sixes promise that you will soon be in touch with a very generous person. If they come up with the card representing 'yourself', you are being very generous.

Seven of Clubs

This card is one of the best in the pack. It stands for victory.

If you are concerned as to the result of any business, or affair, or contest, you may confidently expect the very best.

If reversed, its meaning is not quite so good, the significance, then being financial worry; but note that this is not loss or even disappointment, only worry; at worst, it is delay which causes the worry.

Clubs are always good in relation to business inquiries, though they do not mean things are easy to come by. This card promises no mere good luck, but victory by your own efforts.

Eight of Clubs

This card promises you the help of a good friend or ally, of the opposite sex to your own.

In the 'fortune' of a business man, this Eight of Clubs, if there is a King or Kings near it, may mean a new partner in business. However, when reversed it tells of a warning against speculation, a warning which a real friend has already given you.

If it comes near black cards or Hearts, your new friend is a person either of dark or of light-brown complexion; with Diamonds near, he or she will be fair or grey.

This Eight of Clubs is a happy sign for lovers in distress. It tells of the goodwill of a friend able and willing to help. Reversed, it shows one not so powerful, though very willing to make the course of true love run more smoothly.

Nine of Clubs

This card tells you that you are going to hear of a legacy or of some business following the validation of a will. If it is cut reversed, it speaks of delayed and troubled journeys, generally after or connected with a death or a funeral.

With the Jack of Spades, business with a lawyer is promised. With either the King, Queen, or Jack of Diamonds, rivalry in love is sure to crop up.

To an unmarried man or woman, this card, if cut, says: 'Do not act against the wishes of your friends.' However, to the married and to all those who are concerned with business or with secret affairs, the contrary advice is indicated: 'Take no advice but your own and you will do well.'

Ten of Clubs

This is a very good card to cut if business affairs are engrossing you. It says: 'Cease to worry.' Things are going better than you fear. It does not promise a dramatically good change, but a sure and certain improvement. 'The slow success is the sure success'– especially in business.

This card often foretells of a journey, concerned with good business rather than pleasure. With the other black Ten, a voyage is certain, and successful if red cards are around these two black ones.

All Clubs signify ambition, success which has been slow and difficult to come by, manhood, decisiveness, and the more masculine qualities of the mind.

Two Tens indicate a change of trade. Two red Tens say a lucky and surprising change concerning your business. Three Tens stand for prosperity and the promise of a happy future.

Jack of Clubs

It is very lucky indeed to cut this card at any time. To a dark young girl, it promises a faithful lover and a marriage founded on true friendship and mutual esteem. To a dark young bachelor, it says: 'Go on as you are now doing. You are surely working towards success.' If an older, dark man cuts it, or if it comes in a fortune told him, this Jack of Clubs bids him follow out the thought which at present grips him; in short, to act on his own initiative. An older, married woman who cuts the Jack of Clubs will hear gratifying news of her son's success.

For those who are not of the dark-brown complexion of which Clubs are the signification, this Jack of Clubs says that a friend is thinking about them and they will certainly hear of him – a hasty, big-hearted friend; not necessarily a man friend, but a very true one of either sex.

If a brown-eyed person's fortune is being read, the seer may make the card that particular person's 'thoughts', and if carefully noting the cards around this one, will be able to tell much of the hopes, aspirations and ambitions, as distinct from the actual events in the subject's life, at the time.

Queen of Clubs

If you are a dark-eyed, brown-haired girl or woman, it is very lucky to cut this card, for it signifies 'yourself'. It says: 'Go in and win! Be bold, be bold, and evermore be bold!' You will surely come out on top, whatever tight corner you are in.

If you are a man of this colouring, the omen is lucky in regard to love. For whatever the colouring of the woman you love might be, this card stands for her; she is your Queen and she is thinking sweet thoughts of you. However, if reversed, you have offended her or she is unhappy; ensure that you rectify this situation as soon as possible.

King of Clubs

It is always lucky to cut this card because the Clubs stand for successful efforts and Kings are powerful helpers.

The Club Picture Cards signify good friends rather than lovers, unless you are a dark woman (Queen of Clubs). This card reversed means that your powerful friend is worried or hindered – not quite so powerful on your behalf. With Spades near there is trouble between you. If a man holds it with the Queen near, a powerful partnership is suggested; with the wish card (Nine of Hearts) near, great success throughout the year. If cut with the Ten of Hearts, then marriage with someone you now regard as a friend is indicated. This last applies to either a man or a woman.

Ace of Clubs

This card signifies important papers, written plans, shares, contracts, leases – lucky, successful papers, in fact, rather than mere letters. Good business letters may be indicated.

If reversed, this card means a delay to written prospects or a delay over signed papers, with perhaps some anxiety as to the outcome.

However, unless surrounded by Spades, even if the Ace is reversed, it does not necessarily mean unpleasant communications regarding business.

Clubs always refer to ability, merit, and things that have been earned or deserved.

Fortune Telling by Dominoes

Each small oblong domino has a secret meaning. It is a simple matter to commit these to memory; and in this, as in other methods of divination, the fundamental principle is that of comparison and calculation.

The dominoes used range from double-six to double-blank, and these symbolise the various conditions of fate likely to befall mankind. The exponent places the dominoes on the table, and, having turned them face down proceeds to shuffle them. When this is done, the subject is requested to draw three pieces, one at a time. Between the choice of each, the dominoes should be shuffled.

The first supplies an impression; should it be drawn a second time, the impression becomes a conviction. The third, however, may lessen or wholly contradict its degree of importance, and this is where calculation and comparison in blending the signs are essential to a successful justification and interpretation of these symbols.

Do not draw more than three pieces at a single consultation or you may well find that interpretations are misleading.

Double-six is an emblem of matrimonial happiness and financial prosperity.

Six-five is almost equally fortunate. Perseverance and concentration are rewarded by ultimate success.

Six-four implies a comfortable income, and secures happiness in marriage.

Six-three demonstrates that fate smiles upon love and marriage of the subject.

Six-two shows prudence, hard work, and a certain amount of good luck, or exposure and shame for any wrongdoing.

Six-one promises two marriages to the young subject, the first of which will not be as happy as the second. Should the subject be of middle-age, this domino foretells the speedy arrival of good things and the fact that he or she will never be lonely and uncared for.

Six-blank is, unfortunately, a sign of great trouble - sickness, death, or heavy money losses.

Double-five tells that all achievements will be rewarded with a large amount of success, but inordinate wealth is not prophesied.

Five-four is almost as unfortunate a draw as six-blank. Should a young girl lift it, it means that her future husband will be poor and leave her a widow. Further, he may be of extravagant disposition, in spite of his poverty.

Five-three indicates a tranquil and contented existence. Sufficient money and matrimonial affection of moderate strength, the couple being incapable of passionate devotion.

Five-two conveys a warning that love and marriage are destined to an unhappy termination.

Five-one tells of social popularity, but financial worries and losses.

Five-blank is supposed to demonstrate egotistical and avaricious characteristics, tendencies to swindling and intrigues, also a warning to remain unmarried.

Double-four the person who earns a livelihood by manual labour may regard this domino as a sign of future security and prosperity, but to those whose profession needs mental achievement it is rather disastrous. Troubles and disappointments await.

Four-three indicates matrimony and moderate income.

Four-two proclaims an early marriage and moderate income.

Four-one foretells wealth or many friends.

Four-blank is a sure warning that single life will be the best and happiest. It counsels that any secrets imparted to another will be indiscreetly revealed.

Double-three implies enormous riches.

Three-two foretells prosperity in matrimony, travels, and speculations.

Three-one indicates some danger and unhappiness. The necessity for acting with extreme caution in all matters.

Three-blank warns of domestic unhappiness – such as a quarrel or incompatibility of temperament of husband and wife. The absence of harmony in the home.

Double-two promises average happiness and income.

Two-one is a sign of two marriages, if the individual be a woman; financial failures to a commercial man.

Two-blank implies that the intrigues of unscrupulous people will meet with temporary success. It also denotes poverty, and an indolent husband. The individual will return safely from all journeys undertaken.

Double-one foretells an existence free from money worries; peace and constancy in love and marriage.

Double-blank seems to favour the deeds of unprincipled people, and foretells want of integrity in lover and husband.